THE JOHN MUIR TRAIL

THE JOHN MUIR TRAIL

By

Don and Roberta Lowe

The CAXTON PRINTERS, Ltd.
Caldwell, Idaho 83605
1982

© 1982 by
The Caxton Printers, Ltd.
Caldwell, Idaho

Maps Courtesy of
U.S. Geological Survey

Library of Congress Cataloging in Publication Data

Lowe, Don.
  The John Muir Trail.

    Includes index.
    1. Backpacking — California — John Muir Trail
— Guide-books. 2. John Muir Trail (Calif.) —
Guide-books. I. Lowe, Roberta. II. Title.
GV199.42.C22J635   1982   917.94′4   75-28572
ISBN 0-87004-251-3 (pbk.)   AACR2

Lithographed and bound in the United States of America by
The Caxton Printers, Ltd.
Caldwell, Idaho 83605
127331

CONTENTS

ILLUSTRATIONS

INTRODUCTION

Probably the best terrain for backpacking in the U.S. (maybe anywhere) is the Sierra Nevada, that 400-mile-long range that extends from south of Lassen Peak to Walker Pass and forms the backbone of California. A brazen assertion, perhaps, but easily defended. Other regions may be as magnificently scenic — the Colorado Rockies and the North Cascades of Washington come immediately to mind — but nowhere else is there the vast network of trails and possible cross-country routes under such generally beneficent skies and over so many thousands of acres unsullied by roads or other major signs of man's handiwork. Don't be deceived by photos that make the Sierra Nevada look austere, for it never is. Even areas well above timberline have a delicacy about them.

Traversing the length of the High Sierra (as the crème de la crème of the Sierra Nevada is called) through Yosemite, Kings Canyon and Sequoia national parks and the Minarets and John Muir wildernesses, is the John Muir Trail. From Yosemite Valley it heads east and south for 207.5 miles across lush meadows and high alpine tundra, past dainty tarns and uncounted lakes of assorted shapes and sizes, far above timberline over high passes, and through immense valleys and basins rimmed by awesome peaks and ridges to the summit of Mt. Whitney — at 14,500 feet the highest point in the contiguous United States. Although the John Muir Trail officially ends there, an eight-mile trail winds down the eastern escarpment to Whitney Portal and is the logical conclusion of the route. Along with the Pacific Crest Trail (of which it is a part) and the Appalachian Trail, the John Muir is one of *the* classic backpacking routes.

Although John Muir didn't instigate construction of the John Muir Trail, it's entirely appropriate that it was named for him. He first came to Yosemite in 1868, when he was 30 years old, extensively explored the High Sierra, and expressed his observations in sensitive and perceptive books, articles, and lectures. He was instrumental in having Yosemite Valley and the adjacent high country set aside as a national park, organizing the Sierra Club and, through his friendship with Teddy Roosevelt, planting the seeds of the latter's proconservation leanings.

Although others had the notion of a high-elevation traverse along or near the crest of the High Sierra, the specific proposal that resulted in the John Muir Trail was put forth in 1914, the year Muir died. Actual construction — funded by the California State Legislature — began three years later. Much of the northern portion was passable along old Indian and sheep trails. Other routes, particularly along canyon floors, already existed. However, many sections of the proposed route, such as over Muir Pass and across the Kings-Kern Divide at Forester Pass, remained to be built. The trail was completed twenty-one years and $50,000 later. Hal Roth's *Pathway in the Sky* (Howell-North Books, Berkeley, California) gives a detailed — and, needless to say interesting

— history of the John Muir Trail and of earlier treks into the High Sierra during the last quarter of the 1800s.

Another highly recommended book for background reading is *History of the Sierra Nevada* by Francis Farquhar. This is a cultural history of the area and extends in time from the native Indians through the first European explorers and the gold rush to those high-country trekkers of the late 1800s. The standard handbook on plants and animals of the area (and a bit of physical geography) is Storer and Usinger's *Sierra Nevada Natural History*. The complex geologic story of the Sierra is covered more thoroughly in *Geology of the Sierra Nevada* by Mary Hill. Except for the *Pathway* book, all are available in paperback and are published by the University of California Press, Berkeley.

All four books make enjoyable and informative reading both before and after trips into the Sierra, and those on natural history and geology can, of course, be used as field manuals. If these and the many other books on the Sierra, such as the works of John Muir, aren't available in local bookstores or libraries, you can write the Yosemite Natural History Association, P.O. Box 545, Yosemite National Park, California 95389 for its publications catalogue. If you're in Yosemite Valley you can visit the well-stocked bookstore at the Information Center in Yosemite Village.

The John Muir Trail (hereafter referred to as the JMT) actually is only one part of a vast interlocking network of trails in the Sierra. You could spend your entire backpacking life following this plethora of routes. Laterals from the west and, particularly, the east sides enable backpackers to do sections of the JMT if they don't have the time or inclination to make the entire trek. The laterals also are welcome exits when hikers want to escape from particularly foul weather, become lame, or whatever. All these options for exit and entry points and possible side trips mean you have an awesome number of combinations and permutations of routes to work with — actually not an unpleasant amusement on dreary winter evenings.

PAPERWORK

Itinerary

In fact, making plans in the middle of winter for a trek along the JMT is not only a pleasure, it's prudent, primarily because in the Sierra you must have a wilderness permit to backpack (and even for day hikes in the Inyo and Sierra national forests). Although you can try to obtain a permit in person just before you begin any trek, there is a strictly enforced quota at trailheads, so it's definitely preferable to take advantage of the reservation system and apply for your permit months in advance. In either case, you'll need a reasonably precise itinerary before you are issued a permit.

As a supplement to this guide, particularly if you're doing the JMT in sections, you should acquire recreation maps for the Inyo and Sierra national forests. Send one dollar for each map to Inyo National Forest, White Mountain Ranger District, 798 N. Main St., Bishop, California 93514, and Sierra National Forest, Pineridge Ranger District, P.O. Box 300, Shaver Lake, California 93664. Combined, these maps give a good overview of much of the trail system in the High Sierra. Unfortunately, the National Park Service doesn't have comparable maps, but in most cases the Forest Service ones will provide all the information you'll need.

Unless you plan to make cross-country trips well away from the JMT, U.S.

Geological Survey topographic maps aren't necessary. However, if you do want to purchase any, the relevant ones covering the JMT are, from north to south: Yosemite, Tuolumne Meadows, Mono Craters, Devils Postpile, Mt. Morrison, Mt. Abbot, Blackcap Mountain, Mt. Goddard, Big Pine, Mt. Pinchot, Mt. Whitney, and Lone Pine. All have a scale of 15 minutes. If the ones you need aren't available locally you can order them by sending $1.25 for each map with its name, state (California), and scale to: Branch of Distribution, Central Region, U.S. Geological Survey, Box 25286, Denver Federal Center, Denver, Colorado 80225. A state index that shows the terrain each map covers is available from the above address at no cost.

This guide describes the JMT from north to south — primarily because the higher passes are at the southern end and, theoretically, by the time you reach them you should be in better condition and find them easier to cross. Secondly, if you're starting early in the season more snow will have melted by the time you reach them. Of course, you can do the trip in the reverse direction or, as noted earlier, in shorter sections. Assuming you want snow-free passes, you can begin from the northern end after the first of July in a normal year. If you're starting from the southern end you should delay the departure time by about three weeks. The Sierra usually remains snow free, excluding brief storms, until mid-October.

The main exits or entrances, depending on which way you're heading, form the boundaries for the ten sections in this guide, but these are by no means the only laterals. Others are shown on the maps, noted in the short introductory comments for each section, and then described in detail as they are met en route. As a preliminary aid in planning your itinerary, camping restrictions and possible side trips also are mentioned in the section introductions and are discussed more thoroughly in the main text.

Accompanying each map is a cross-sectional profile of the trail. It affords graphic information on the relationship between the distance, the elevation gain (or loss), and the grade of each portion of the JMT. For precise numerical data, refer to the table that lists the mileage points of specific fixes and the elevation gains (or losses) between them. Keep in mind the relationship between distance and elevation gain as you plan each day's travel. As you most likely know, you can comfortably hike farther on a day when the elevation gain is moderate. Conversely, you'll need to shorten the distance if you have considerably more climbing. Covering twenty miles with a gain of four thousand feet might be a fun, hard day-hike, but it would be a mistake to attempt such a feat as part of a backpack. (Overextending yourself to get out before a monstrous snowstorm would be one valid exception to this "take it easy" philosophy.)

Since you'll be traveling at high elevations and with a heavy load, don't plan to cover more than an average of eight to twelve miles per day. If one day has to be particularly hard — for instance, if you have to push to put yourself in position to get over a pass early the next morning because lightning storms are expected — follow it with an easy or rest day. Plan for occasional rest days at outstanding scenic sites; also allow for a couple of unscheduled stops so you can afford to lay over if you feel run down. You're supposed to be having a good time — not shuffling through the High Sierra in introverted agony.

For increased clarity, lakes and streams are shown in black on the maps. Also, throughout the text, physical features are set in bold face type at the point where you actually meet them so you can more easily locate the specific information in the copy. For the same reason, all side trips are set in reduced type to distinguish them quickly from the description of the JMT.

Permits

As noted aleady, free wilderness permits are required for any overnight or longer trips in the High Sierra (and for day hikes in the Inyo and Sierra national forests). These restrictions have been established to protect the terrain and maintain a reasonable wilderness atmosphere for visitors. These measures are sensible, and once you receive your own permit you'll have a personal reason for appreciating the controls on the competition for space.

On any trip in the Sierra, regardless of how many national parks and forests you pass through, you need obtain only one permit per group, and you apply for it at your *point of entry*, either ahead of time — by mail or phone — or in person just before you intend to begin the backpack. The appropriate addresses from which to obtain permits for all but the most exotic approaches to the JMT are listed in the accompanying box.

You will need to provide the following information: Date of entry and exit; location of entry and exit; method of travel; number of people in group; number of pack animals; best estimate of overnight camp areas and number of nights you intend to spend in each; your name and address.

Getting the permit is actually a bit more complicated because of the daily quotas that have been imposed at most of the trailheads. Also, each forest and park has its own system:

Yosemite National Park. Mail applications for permits are accepted from February 1 through May 31 only. Fifty percent of the daily quotas can be filled by mail. Permits for the other half are issued on a first-come, first-served basis upon arrival in the park.

Inyo National Forest (all east side approaches). Two-thirds of the daily quota for each trailhead can be filled by advance registration. There's no time limit for a reservation, but allow enough time for the permit to be processed and mailed back to you — ten days to two weeks.

Sequoia-Kings Canyon National Parks. Same system as for Inyo National Forest except that only 50 percent of the daily trailhead quotas can be reserved.

WHERE TO OBTAIN WILDERNESS PERMITS

YOSEMITE NATIONAL PARK
   Yosemite National Park
   Backcountry Office
   Box 577
   Yosemite, California 95389
      (209) 372-4461, Ext. 85 or 56

EAST SIDE ENTRY
   Silver Lake to Mammoth Lakes
   Inyo National Forest
   Mammoth Ranger District
   Box 148
   Mammoth Lakes, California 93546
      (714) 934-2505

   McGee Creek to South Lake
   Inyo National Forest
   White Mountain Ranger District
   798 N. Main St.
   Bishop, California 93514
      (714) 873-4207

   Taboose Pass to Whitney Portal
   Inyo National Forest
   Mount Whitney Ranger District
   P.O. Box 8
   Lone Pine, California 93545
      (714) 876-4660

WEST SIDE ENTRY
   Edison Lake to Florence Lake
   Sierra National Forest
   Pineridge Ranger District
   P.O. Box 300
   Shaver Lake, California 93664
      (209) 841-3311

   Courtright Reservoir and
   Wishon Reservoir
   Sierra National Forest
   Kings River Ranger District
   Trimmer Route
   Sanger, California 93657
      (209) 855-8321

   Cedar Grove and Wolverton
   Sequoia-Kings Canyon
   National Parks
   Chief Ranger's Office
   Three Rivers, California 93271
      (209) 565-3306

Sierra National Forest. Mail applications for wilderness permits are accepted after March 1. Two-thirds of the daily quota for each trailhead can be filled by mail or phone. Allow three weeks for processing.

Since quotas have been adopted because of high demand, obviously it's recommended that you apply for a permit as early in the season as possible.

However, as noted above, one-half (or one-third in the case of the Inyo and Sierra national forests) of the daily quota for permits is available on a first-come, first-served basis. If you choose to obtain your permit in person, you can get it at the above addresses up to twenty-four hours prior to departure. During the summer months in Yosemite National Park you also can obtain a permit from the station at Tuolumne Meadows, along the road to the ranger station and the High Sierra Camp (Tuolumne Meadows Lodge). The Inyo National Forest also has permit stations open during the summer months west of U.S. 395 along the spur roads to Whitney Portal, the South-Sabrina-North Lakes area, and Rock Creek (the Mono Pass trailhead). Similarly, the Sierra National Forest has summer stations open at Huntington Lake, the High Sierra Ranger Station, and Dinkey Creek. These stations have longer hours than year-around ranger stations in the towns.

If you opt to obtain your permit just before you begin the backpack and the nonreserved portion of the quota already has been filled, you will have to take an alternate route or wait a day or two and try again. Scheduling your entry date for a weekday or after Labor Day will increase your chance of getting a permit for the date and trailhead you want.

In general, large groups are not encouraged in the wildernesses. In the Inyo National Forest no more than one-third of the daily quota for a trailhead may be reserved by a group of ten or more. Groups of fifteen or more entering Yosemite National Park are requested to apply for a reservation at least two weeks in advance of the departure date.

Logistics

The main problem with any backpack lasting more than two weeks is carrying enough food — and to do the entire JMT takes three to four weeks. People who are experienced, disciplined (i.e. tolerant of deprivation), swift-moving, and perhaps a bit lucky have managed to pack sufficient sustenance for the entire trek. Of course, if you travel with someone else so the tent, cookware, and such can be shared, the above is much more feasible. Alternatives include mailing food to pack stations and resorts at the beginning of some of the feeder trails, packing in caches before starting the trek proper, finagling friends to hike in with supplies at predetermined points, or taking laterals to the towns along U.S. 395. For some people these trips out to roads, autos, frenzy, and noise are a welcome change, but for most it's a nerve-wracking contrast to the relative peace of the backcountry. Because of the comparative shortness of the trails down the east side (and the good-sized town of Bishop and smaller Independence, Big Pine, and Lone Pine along U.S. 395) you should plan to head that way for supplies rather than to the west.

A final alternative, not encouraged, is having a packer bring supplies to a predetermined spot. Those who do this charge at least $50, but as you travel in the Sierra and see the damage done by stock travel, you'll most likely agree you wouldn't want to add to this destruction. For information on the location and facilities of the resorts and packers on the east side write the Chamber of Commerce, Box 147, Bishop, California 93514. For information on packers, and resorts on the west side refer to the recreation map for the Sierra National Forest, which lists these services.

If you enjoy fishing and hope to supplement your diet, you'll need a California state license. Although fishing can be good in places, it's better to be conservative when you plan your commissary and assume that it won't be.

BACKPACKING IN THE SIERRA

This guide doesn't discuss backpacking techniques in general, since several fine books are available that cover the subject in detail. One of the best is *Backpacking — One Step At A Time* by Harvey Manning, published by The REI Press, Seattle, Washington. It's available in paperback from the Yosemite Natural History Association in Yosemite National Park, mentioned earlier. However, a few specific comments about backpacking in the Sierra Nevada should be noted:

One of the Sierra's sobriquets is "The Gentle Wilderness," and usually it has moderate day and night temperatures and long stretches of perfect weather. But there are occasional afternoon thunderstorms, plain old frontal systems can bring rains, and, as in all high country, sudden summer blizzards of appalling intensity can dump up to several feet of snow. With few exceptions, those who suffer, and sometimes perish, in inclement weather are those who (a) didn't have the proper gear — specifically, a good mountain tent with a rain fly, adequate clothing (including long pants) to keep warm, a waterproof cover for the pack, and a poncho — and (b) didn't have enough skills to use (a) properly. Although it is extra weight and may elicit stares from fellow travelers, an umbrella is an excellent way to keep dry while traveling or standing around camp. Ponchos are necessary while doing chores, but if you wear them while hiking you're likely to get as wet from perspiration as from precipitation.

Unlike lightning storms in many mountainous areas — the Colorado Rockies, for instance — those in the Sierra have the good manners to build reasonably slowly and dissipate soon enough that your gear usually can dry before sunset. Nevertheless, the Sierra variety are potentially dangerous, so you should be off passes and below the high treeless basins before they break. If you place your camps so you can get over the passes by noon you'll usually beat the fireworks. Lightning storms are most prevalent in August, but that doesn't mean they won't occur at other times. Nor should you expect daily ones, even at the height of their season.

Skies are mostly clear, and this abundance of sunlight is intensified by the high elevation, the many miles of travel above timberline, and the reflective nature of the granite rock (the reason the Sierra also is called the "Range of Light"). You should take precautions against all this glare and ultraviolet light by wearing sunglasses and a brimmed hat, and by using a cream with some sort of sun block on nose tip, lips, and the backs of the hands. People with especially sensitive skin or a low tolerance for sun will want to don a lightweight, long-sleeved shirt and gloves after they've gotten their daily dose of vitamin D.

In addition to the weather, the Sierra has other traits that make it a gentle wilderness. Despite the abundance of streams and rivers, crossings seldom are a problem since most of the potentially troublesome ones are bridged. These structures may detract from the wilderness ambience, but aesthetic's loss is safety's gain. There are several ways you can ford unspanned flows that are too deep to cross without getting your feet wet. (The deepest of these, by the way, is seldom above knee height.) The preferred method is to take off boots and socks and wade across in your camp tennies. If possible, fasten your boots to your pack so you won't accidently drop them in the flow. Or you can take off your boots and wear your socks across; or the reverse; or splash across with both on. Take them off on the other side, drain the boots, and wring out the socks. A short distance of hiking in wet boots and socks can be coolingly comfortable, but don't do it for too long as your skin will soften and blisters may form. Crossing in bare feet is not recommended, as they could be severely cut or bruised. Don't get the idea that every stream will necessitate going through one of these rituals. In fact, most of the fords are shallow or narrow enough that you won't have any trouble staying dry.

Although it does add extra weight, it's a good idea to travel with half a bottle of drinking water. This is not to imply the Sierra is arid, for it is not. It's just that along the route there are stretches of a few miles where water is not easily available, and your body should be kept hydrated. Because the atmosphere is so dry, your water (and concurrent salt) losses will be less obvious. People who normally consume little salt may need to increase their intake while backpacking. The usual symptoms of salt deficiency are general muscle fatigue and, eventually, dizziness and nausea. If you stop and slowly take about one-quarter teaspoon of salt with plenty of water you should feel fine again in ten or fifteen minutes. If you don't improve this quickly, something else is wrong.

A final comment on water: If you obtain your drinking water from streams that do not come from lakes, you shouldn't have any gastrointestinal problems. This proscription doesn't apply when you are well away from populated areas. Because of past improper camping techniques at some of the popular lakes, water from them may be contaminated, and you'll most likely want to treat it. Check with a ranger about suspect areas.

Acclimatizing to the high elevations of the Sierra shouldn't be much of a problem if you start from Yosemite Valley or the northern section, take it easy, and are in good shape to begin with. Some people may feel lethargic for a few days. Beginning from Whitney Portal may cause greater suffering, as you'll reach the highest point on the JMT (Mt. Whitney) after only ten miles. Interestingly, some recent medical research indicates that the body begins producing more red blood cells more quickly when "shocked" into doing so. In other words, you may be able to acclimatize in a day or two, rather than several, by abruptly getting to a high elevation rather than moseying up to it.

Mosquitoes are a bane in most of the outdoors, and the Sierra is no exception. You can avoid most, if not all, of them if you plan your visit after mid-August. However, as noted earlier, thunderstorms are more prevalent then — so chose your own poison. Even if you visit later in the season, carry repellent spray for clothing and cream for skin, just in case.

The usual assortment of squirrels and chipmunks (and in some places uncommonly intelligent marmots) are interested in gnawing through your pack and sampling its contents. Less easily put off and considerably more serious are the food-stealing bears that prowl the JMT all through Yosemite National Park, around Thousand Island Lake, from Woods Creek to Charlotte Lake, and, most recently, in the Wallace Creek and Crabtree areas. As you progress along the JMT you can check with rangers and fellow travelers about any new areas bears have invaded. So far they have not been a problem in Sequoia-Kings Canyon National Parks north of Pinchot Pass.

Assuming you don't provoke them, these bears, fortunately, don't care tiddly-pooh about you. The last grizzly in the Sierra was killed in the mid-1920s, a deed not often lamented. The remaining brown bears are interested in your food and are most adept at getting it if you don't follow the proper deterrents. At night and when you're away from camp in bear country, put ALL your food and any cosmetics in a stuff sack or two. Look for a branch at least four inches thick where it joins the trunk and twenty feet off the ground. Some camp areas have steel cables permanently installed between trees. Tie one end of a twelve-foot rope to your stuff sack. Toss the other end over the limb and pull the sack up to near the branch. Tie a counterweight (rock or a second stuff bag) to the other end of the line and, using a stick, adjust the two bundles so they are next to each other and situated fifteen feet from the ground, five feet below the limb, and ten feet from the trunk. Be sure to tie on a couple of metal cups or similar noisemakers to alert you if a bear is jiggling the ropes or bags. If the bear is not about to be shooed away or has succeeded in getting your food, leave him absolutely alone.

As a matter of fact, never touch or get familiar with any wild animal. Even adorable little rodents can carry nasty diseases such as bubonic plague, and you wouldn't want to be scratched or bitten by one. Be especially leery of sick animals — rabies and all that. Although rattlesnakes may be encountered along a few of the laterals, particularly at lower elevations on the west side, you don't have to watch out for them along the JMT once you get beyond Little

Yosemite Valley (and it's highly unlikely that you'll encounter one even along that stretch).

THE "NO TRACE" ETHIC

The tragic flaw of the Sierra Nevada in general and the JMT in particular is that their charms are well known. It's possible to see only a few people a day along the more remote sections, but this is a luxury you can't count on. Fortunately, the open, expansive nature of the terrain tends to minimize the psychological impact of other visitors. The best time to start the backpack, if you want to lessen your contact with other humans, is after Labor Day. You'll have nippier nights and mornings and a greater chance for snow, but the scenery is just as lovely. The next best option is to avoid the most popular (i.e., the most accessible) stretches on weekends. These sections include the first several miles of the JMT up from Yosemite Valley, Tuolumne Meadows, Devils Postpile, Bishop Pass, Kearsarge Pass, and the final eight miles of the JMT between Trail Crest and the end at Whitney Portal.

Blessedly, most of the backpackers who get beyond the first several miles of any trailhead are remarkably well mannered and unobtrusive. This minimum impact on the land and fellow visitors is essential, both for protection of the terrain and to provide the wilderness experience visitors are hoping to find in the backcountry. The forest and park services have catchy phrases for this ethic of inconspicuousness, the favored one currently being "no trace camping." You probably practice many of its tenets already.

Paradoxically, the advances in lightweight camping equipment that abetted the quantum surge in the number of wilderness visitors over the last fifteen years also makes this "no trace camping" easier. Waterproof tent floors and foam pads negate the need to dig trenches and hip holes or to cut boughs. Primus (or similar) stoves eliminate the necessity for wood fires that scar the soil. The attendant rock rings detract from the wilderness ambience, as does any evidence or man's handiwork — not to mention the gleaning of every fallen limb and twig for fuel or the heinous act of cutting into standing trees, living or dead. Not only is much of the terrain in the Sierra Nevada, particularly the High Sierra, sensitive to the cumulative damage from wood fires, but regulations in several specific areas and the absence of adequate wood at and above timberline absolutely preclude fires. Plan to use your stove most, if not all, of the time and carry adequate fuel. When you're camping in areas where wood fires are permitted, try to learn from a ranger ahead of time whether you should use established fire rings or build, and then carefully obliterate, temporary ones.

Where you establish camp is just as important as how you treat the terrain after you locate your site. As tempting as they are — and as popular as they seem to be for ad campaigns — lake and stream shores and grassy areas absolutely cannot withstand the repeated compaction of tents and shuffling feet. Establish camp at least 100 feet from water and in the woods, if possible, or at least away from soft, grassy areas. If you scrape away cones and/or rocks before pitching a tent, scatter them back after you break camp so the site looks more natural. Never construct any permanent features, such as shelves. As is obvious by now, the point of "no trace camping" is exactly what the slogan says: There should be no evidence that you've passed through the area.

As you plan your menu, remember that containers have to be packed out as well as in. This includes cans, glass, plastic, foil, egg shells, and orange rinds, and also paper where fires aren't allowed. Remember that FOIL DOES NOT BURN. Pack it out. If you had room for a container when it was full, you'll have room for it empty. Litter is pleasingly minimal along wilderness trails in the West — much of what there is comes from people who grossly overestimate foil's combustibility or the decomposition rate of shells and rinds. Even with the care most people take, little mistakes add up: If you're impressed by statistics, ten to fifteen thousand pounds of trash are removed from the Sequoia-Kings Canyon backcountry every year.

Disposing of body waste is a bit more complicated. Go to a spot well away from any water source (at least 200 feet) and dig a hole about eight inches deep, keeping the sod intact if possible. A small garden trowel or a large spoon is a good tool. After use, refill the hole with earth and tamp in the sod. Some foresters think the preferable technique above timberline, where soil doesn't promote rapid decomposition, is to leave excrement exposed so it will quickly dry. Where fires are permitted, you can burn the toilet paper at camp. Protect water sources by not cleaning fish, clothes, yourself, or your cooking and eating utensils in them. Collect water and move 100 feet or more away to perform these chores.

The above are obvious aspects of "no trace camping," and most people practice them, but there are also less blatant, though equally important, actions. For instance: Stay on the official trail. Anyone who shortcuts switchbacks can be pegged immediately as an outdoor dummy. This can be dangerous to people traveling below, particularly in places like the rocky Sierra, and it always promotes unsightly erosion channels. Government agencies can put their trail funds to better use than repairing damage that shouldn't have happened in the first place. Also, stay on the tread if the trail has been rerouted, such as they now are above or around (instead of through) meadows or when crossing wet areas or snow patches, even though a short bypass might be a little easier. On a backpack you'll probably be wearing tennies around camp for the benefit of your feet, but these lightweight shoes also spare the ground. (Tennies may also be sufficient for some of your day hikes.)

Since just two or three people, even when careful to minimize their impact, have a noticeable effect on the places they visit, consider what a large group does. And a herd of humans isn't pleasing to others. After all, sheep haven't been allowed in the Sierra backcountry since special dispensation was granted during World War I. Do your part by never being a member of a horde.

Following these practices on where and how to camp will minimize the long-lasting impact on the land and improve the wilderness experience of transient human visitors. But people also deserve respect beyond not having to see abused terrain, and this consideration is part of the "no trace" ethic. One of the most offensive encounters a backpacker or hiker can have is that of aural pollution. Except for a few appalling exceptions, no one brings radios, etc., into the outdoors, and most people have enough manners not to shout, whistle, and otherwise be raucous. But what about that flute someone is tooting? Those nearby probably would prefer to hear the natural sound of the wind through the trees or the water's flow.

About 45 percent of the JMT is through national parks where canines (and felines, for that matter) are absolutely prohibited. Anyone who has rounded a corner to be greeted by an aggressive dog defending what he perceives to be his domain, or has been kept awake by a barking one, no doubt agrees with this ban and feels it might be appropriate on forest service land, too. The absence of dogs is one reason you'll see so much wildlife while you travel through the parks.

Actually, "no trace camping" is a simpler way to enjoy the outdoors and, except for those who enjoy making everything they do as complex as possible, this opportunity to exist at a basic level for a while is one of the lures of backpacking. Like most actions, following the ethic easily becomes a habit, and the old ways will be unlamented. Adhering to the "no trace" camping and hiking ethic shows respect for the land and for fellow visitors. On a less lofty note, you might consider that, although remaining inconspicuous may not always keep you free in the outside world, in the backcountry it may prevent you from getting a citation.

The JMT travels through federal lands managed by either the National Park Service or the U.S. Forest Service. If you have questions, suggestions, complaints, or compliments about how the area is being administered, write to the appropriate agency. For information on conservation issues, contact the Sierra Club, 530 Bush Street, San Francisco, California 94108. If the club is not directly involved in a particular issue that concerns you, you'll be referred to a group that is. Comments intended for the authors can be sent to them in care of The Caxton Printers, Ltd., P.O. Box 700, Caldwell, Idaho 83605.

D.L.
R.L.

YOSEMITE VALLEY TO TUOLUMNE MEADOWS

The jostling crowds that surge around you for the first six miles or so of the John Muir Trail (hereafter referred to as the JMT) aren't welcome, but, all aspects considered, it's about the best place to have to tolerate them. Your wilderness sensibilities haven't yet been heightened, and the bold scenery is completely capable of holding its own against these mere, wee humans, regardless of their numbers.

Early on you'll be passing the well-publicized landmarks of Vernal and Nevada falls and Half Dome. You can make a short side trip up to the summit of the latter from the 6.1-mile point. All along this section you'll see many dramatic examples of how glaciation has shaped the landscape of the Sierra — the massive smooth domes, the jagged summits in the Cathedral Peak area, and the glacial polish and erratics around Tuolumne Meadows. As John Muir prowled through the Sierra he made careful observations and was the first to write about the great extent to which glaciation affected the range.

Side Trips. Nowhere else along the route do you have the option of so many side loops, most of which leave the JMT at, or a short distance above, Little Yosemite Valley. From the junction of the trail to Merced Lake at 4.4 miles you can continue east past Lost Valley and rejoin the JMT at 9.1, 14.7, or 29.6 miles. Although *no* route in the Sierra is without its charms, the only alternative among these three that has special merit is the third option past Merced Lake and up Fletcher Creek through the Vogelsang area. In addition to the fine scenery you'll avoid the hordes at Tuolumne Meadows — assuming you want to avoid them and the services there. Besides the climb of Half Dome, you also can make a side loop to the equally impressive summit of Clouds Rest.

Exit. The only exit along this section that would be shorter than continuing along the JMT to Tuolumne Meadows is the Forsyth Trail to Tenaya Lake, which leaves the main route at 9.1 miles.

Tuolumne Meadows and Reds Meadow, a few days farther on at 56.5 miles, are the only two places along the JMT where you can buy supplies, mail letters, and have "real" food. A luxurious option to tenting is the High Sierra Camp at Sunrise (and Merced Lake and Vogelsang if you're making one of the side loops) where you pay $43 (1982 prices) for dinner, night's lodging, and breakfast. A similar camp at Tuolumne Meadows operates on the European plan. The camps fill quickly so, if you're definitely intending to visit one or more, get your reservations in as soon as possible after November 30. Write the Yosemite Park and Curry Company, Yosemite National Park, California 95389 (phone 209-373-4171).

Camping Restrictions. Since no camping is allowed within a four-mile radius of Yosemite Valley, the first chance for an overnight stay along the JMT is in Little Yosemite Valley, at designated sites only. Within the park wood fires aren't permitted above 9,600 feet, which is between the 15.7 and 17.5-mile points along this section. As noted earlier, food-stealing bears are a problem all through Yosemite National

Park, so observe the appropriate precautions described in the introduction.

Take a shuttle bus or walk to **Happy Isles** at the southeast corner of Yosemite Valley, cross the wide bridge over the Merced River, and come to a large sign listing many mileages. Climb, along with masses of day-hikers, on the paved trail that traverses the steep canyon wall. The laurel and maple trees and kindred vegetation you pass here will be a mix you'll encounter nowhere else along the JMT. At 1.0 mile recross the Merced River and pass above the toilet facilities. The fountain here provides the last dependable and easily accessible drinking water for 3.4 miles. One-tenth mile farther come to the junction of the **Mist Trail**. The distinctive cutout metal trail signs (animal-proof) are unique to Yosemite

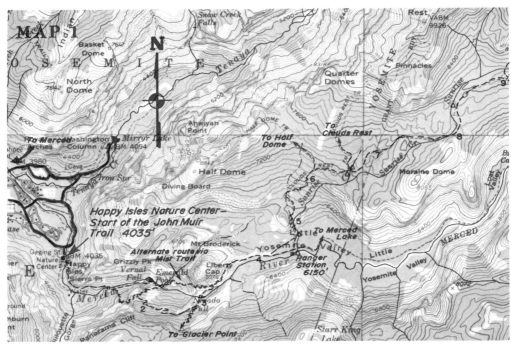

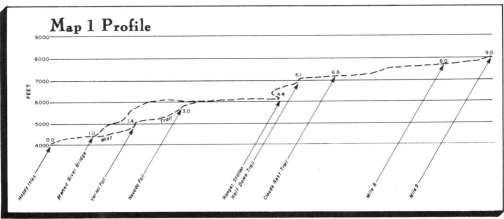

Liberty Cap and Nevada Fall

National Park. By the time you reach Donohue Pass on the southern boundary you'll consider them quaint old friends.

The Mist Trail rejoins the JMT a short distance northeast of Nevada Fall. Although shorter by one mile, this wonderfully scenic side loop is not recommended for backpackers because (a) the section below Vernal Fall leads up stone steps with high risers that would be much extra work for someone with a heavy load and (b) through midsummer you'd most likely get soaked with spray from Vernal Fall. The latter is no problem for hikers; on a sunny day they'll dry off before they reach Nevada Fall. Backpackers' equipment won't fare so well. If you do opt to take this attractive, interesting route, keep straight at the junction and soon begin climbing the stone steps to the fenced overlook at **Vernal Fall**. Walk down the rock slabs toward the river, then turn sharply right several yards before the flow. Climb at about a thirty-degree angle away from the river along a maddeningly obscure tread and, after a few hundred feet, look for one of the metal signs stating Nevada Fall 1.3 miles. Continue up along the trail for a few yards to a junction and turn left. The tread to the right switchbacks for 0.6 mile up to the JMT. To continue along the Mist Trail, turn left and walk over a cobblestone-like surface to the third bridge over the Merced River. Travel through fairly open terrain, eventually pass toilet facilities to your left along a level stretch, enter deep woods, and come near the base of **Nevada Fall**. The trail becomes increasingly rocky and rises in short switchbacks to the top of the cliff and the junction with the JMT. The lip of the fall is about 0.2 mile to the right.

To follow the JMT from the lower junction of the Mist Trail at 1.1 miles, turn right and switchback up through woods for about 1.0 mile and then travel through more open terrain that affords good views. The peaks to the north across the Merced River are, from left to right, Grizzly Peak, Half Dome, Mt. Broderick, and Liberty Cap. Farther on you'll be able to see the Pinnacles and Clouds Rest. At 1.7 miles come to the junction of the connector to the Mist Trail and the top of Vernal Fall. Keep right and traverse gradually

uphill for 1.0 mile to the junction of the trail that passes Panorama Point and eventually ends at Glacier Point. Stay left on the main route and descend slightly for 0.2 mile to the bridge over the Merced River at **Nevada Fall**. Cross the span, and 0.2 mile farther keep right at the junction of the high end of the Mist Trail.

After short stretches of uphill, level, and downhill, walk at an almost level grade near the Merced River along a tread that, beyond Nevada Fall, has become blessedly smooth. The fairly open cover of manzanita and a few pines and cedars eventually is replaced by deeper woods. Come to the west end of **Little Yosemite Valley.** The path to the left at a fork forms the hypotenuse of a triangle and rejoins the JMT a short distance north of the ranger station. Continue on the level for 0.3 mile to the ranger station, toilet facilities, the first camping area, and, a short distance farther, the signed junction of the trail to Merced Lake.

This is the point from which you begin three of the side loops mentioned earlier. The shortest is to follow the trail toward Merced Lake for 6.0 miles to Echo Valley. Turn left onto the signed trail to Sunrise High Sierra Camp and after a short distance turn left again onto a lateral trail that will lead you back to a junction with the JMT at 9.1 miles. Or you can continue on the trail from Echo Valley to Sunrise, climbing to Long Meadow and rejoining the JMT at the 14.7-mile point. The most scenic way, as noted before, is to climb from Merced Lake to Vogelsang, following either the route along Fletcher Creek or the one that parallels Lewis Creek. From Vogelsang, cross a treeless slope of low-growing grass that is home for an impressive population of Belding ground squirrels, pass Evelyn Lake, and descend to the Lyell Fork valley and the junction with the JMT at 29.6 miles.

To continue along the JMT, keep left at the junction as indicated by signs, enjoy the last of the level grade for several miles, and resume climbing through a forest of incense cedar and pine. The tread is rocky for only a short

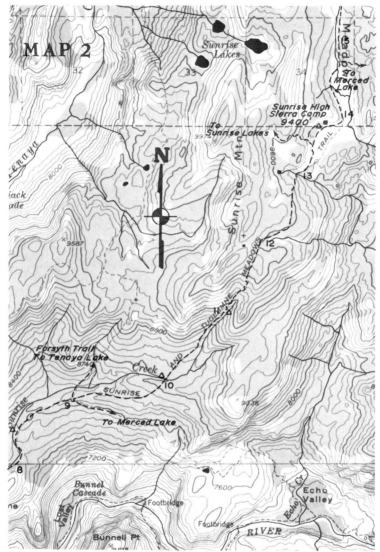

MAP 2

Sunrise Lakes

To Merced Lake

Sunrise High Sierra Camp 9400' 14

13

12

Forsyth Trail To Tenaya Lake

Creek 10

SUNRISE 9

To Merced Lake

8

Bunnel Cascade

Footbridge

Footbridge RIVER

Echo Valley

Bunnell Pt

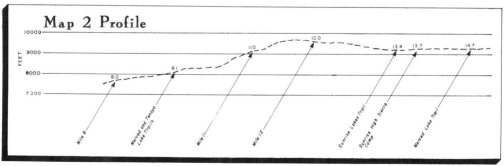

Map 2 Profile

10000

9000

FEET

8000

7500

8.0   9.1   11.0   12.0   13.4   13.7   14.7

Mile 8   Merced and Tenaya Lake Trails   Mile 11   Mile 12   Sunrise Lakes Trail   Sunrise High Sierra Camp   Merced Lake Trail

distance. Continue switchbacking up, and at 6.1 miles come to the junction of the trail to Half Dome, whose distinctive silhouette is used as a logo for Yosemite National Park.

The round trip to Half Dome involves an additional 4.0 miles and 1,900 feet of elevation gain. The last 700 feet up the smooth rock slope to the broad summit, with its views of Yosemite and Little Yosemite valleys, Tenaya Canyon, and the peripheral peaks and domes, is made possible by cable handlines and wooden slats bolted to the rock. Don't attempt this final pitch if the cable isn't up (a ranger can tell you whether it is) or when a lightning storm is threatening. If you should be caught on the cable during a sudden storm, hang on to only one line until the danger passes. If you were grasping both lines when a lightning bolt hit, the current might pass through your body. If the shock didn't kill you, the fall surely would.

Even if you can't — or don't want to — make the final pitch to the summit, you'll still be scenically rewarded by the side trip, as the view from the base of the cable route is excellent.

To follow the trail to Half Dome, turn left, continue climbing, and then level off at a ridge crest. Descend slightly to the base of a subsidiary hump that, despite its appearance, presents no problem, and then drop slightly to the saddle at the base of the final pitch up the cable route.

The JMT traverses along a more open area of pines, manzanita, and boulders. For the next 7.5 miles, until reaching Sunrise High Sierra Camp, you should encounter considerably fewer people. One-half mile from the Half Dome junction come to the trail to Clouds Rest, the highest point in the immediate Yosemite Valley area.

Because of its location, elevation, and lack of obstructing vegetation, the view from Clouds Rest is panoramic, extending over Tenaya Lake and the slopes and peaks of the entire northern High Sierra. The side trip to this viewpoint involves an extra 4.0 miles one-way and 2,750 feet of uphill. Instead of retracing your route back to the JMT you can follow a section of the trail to Tenaya Lake to a junction, turn right, descend, and rejoin the JMT at its 9.1-mile point. To make the side trip, keep left, climb through woods for a mile,

and then switchback up the brush-covered slope below the Pinnacles. Pass through an open, rocky area and then continue up through woods to a junction. You'll follow the route here on the return trip if you want to rejoin the JMT at 9.1 miles. Turn left and climb the final 0.4 mile to Clouds Rest.

At 125 feet from the Clouds Rest junction come to a camp near a stream, the first good source of water since leaving the Merced River. Cross it, and after a short level stretch resume climbing and travel near **Sunrise Creek**. Eventually cross it, continue paralleling the flow, and then veer away as the trail grade steepens. Level off and then rise gradually to the junction of the connector that leaves the trail to Merced Lake at Echo Valley. Keep left, and 100 yards farther come to the junction of the Forsyth Trail to Tenaya Lake. This is the route you could have taken back to the JMT if you'd made the side loop to Clouds Rest.

Stay right and continue climbing. You can see all three peaks of Mt. Starr King to the south, look southeast to Mt. Clark, or, by turning around, gaze back to Half Dome and Sentinel Dome. Traverse along the not too densely wooded slope and have fine views down into the immense Merced River valley. Drop briefly, walk on the level for a short distance, and then climb an erratic grade ranging from gradual to moderately steep. Be sure to fill your water bottles at the crossing of Sunrise Creek at 10.0 miles or at some point along the next mile as there are no more good sources until Sunrise High Sierra Camp at 13.7 miles. Come to an interesting crest of rocks, trees, and sparse ground cover near 11.7 miles and begin descending the other side.

As you pass above a meadow you can see east to Mts. Florence, Lyell, and McClure. Here you first see the spires of Cathedral and Echo peaks ahead to the north. You can walk a few hundred

Trail sign above Little Yosemite Valley

feet to the right off the trail for a view of the southwestern tip of Long Meadow. Continue downhill through woods, and 1.5 miles from the crest come to the corner of Long Meadow and the junction of a connector to Sunrise and Tenaya lakes. Although circuitous, you could have rejoined the JMT along this route from the side trip to Clouds Rest. Keep straight and after 400 yards pass the signed path that

goes up for a couple of hundred feet to **Sunrise High Sierra Camp,** whose amenities were described in the introduction to this section.

Continue along the edge of the immense meadow and, as you curve left, have a second sighting of the spires of Cathedral Peak and, closer by, Columbia Finger and Tresidder Peak. You'll eventually pass near all three. Continue skirting the edge of Long

Cathedral Peak

Meadow, and 1.0 mile from Sunrise High Sierra Camp come to the junction of the second connector from the trail to Merced Lake.

Keep straight (left), enter an area of small trees, cross a stream, and continue uphill. Pass through a meadow, curve northeast into deeper woods, and begin winding up at a more noticeable grade. Traverse the south side of **Columbia Finger** and then, after a short section of level and downhill, make the final climb to a boulder-strewn crest that has no official name but is, in fact, 220 feet higher than Cathedral Pass, which you'll shortly be crossing. Good views from here to the south and, closer by, Echo, Cathedral and Coxcomb peaks.

Traverse downhill along the wooded east slope of **Tresidder Peak** for 0.5 mile to the north end of a meadow and cross it to 9,700-foot **Cathedral Pass** — certainly a lovely spot but hardly worthy of the designation when compared to the monsters you'll be crossing farther along the JMT. From the crest you'll be able to look over Upper Cathedral Lake, where the best camping is at the northeast and north ends. Descend

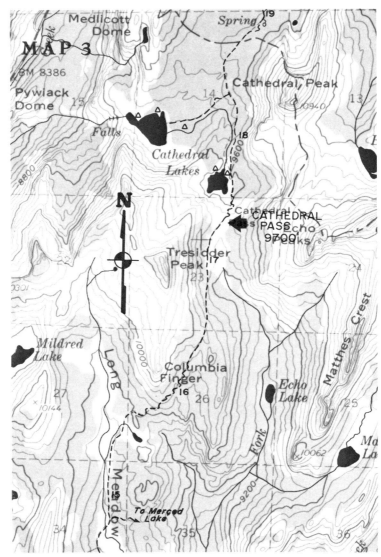

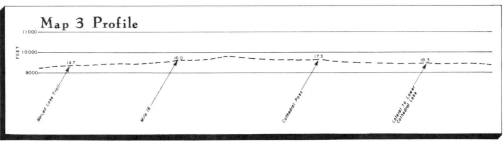

Map 3 Profile

from the pass to a large, lush meadow and walk on the level, passing near **Upper Cathedral Lake**. Enter woods and descend for 0.5 mile to the junction of the 0.5-mile spur to Lower Cathedral Lake.

To reach Lower Cathedral Lake, about twice as large as its higher sibling, wind down, losing about 200 feet, to a small clearing. Cross it, then cross a considerably larger one, and come to the eastern shore. The best campsites are on the north side.

Follow the sign pointing to Tuolumne Meadows. After two short climbs separated by a level stretch begin winding downhill through woods. Cross a creek (the first easily accessible water since Sunrise High Sierra Camp that doesn't have a good possibility of being polluted by stock) and a short distance farther pass through a small meadow. Walk on the level along a stretch that can be a bit boggy, make one final climb, and then descend — passing the unsigned junction of the trail to Budd Lake — to a four-way junction. From here you have the option of taking the dogleg route along the official JMT, paralleling the road past the post office, store, and coffee shop, or of skirting all the chaos by bearing right and

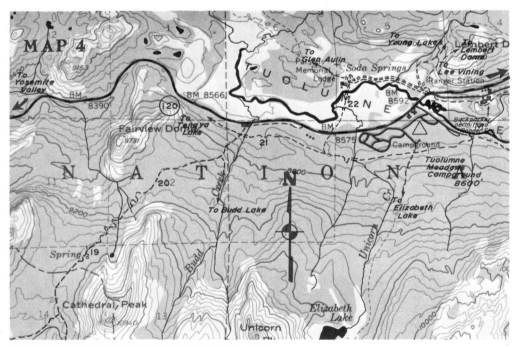

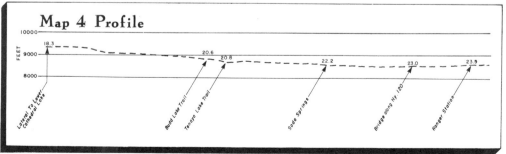

traversing through woods to the junction with the JMT at 24.9 miles. The price you pay for saving 1.5 miles and avoiding the congestion is missing much of the fine, expansive scenery of Tuolumne Meadows. Refer ahead to Section B for a description of this detour.

Keep straight, and after 0.1 mile come to the **Tioga Road**. Turn right and walk along the trail that parallels the south shoulder. (Continue along the road if you want to visit any of the above facilities.) To remain on the official JMT, cross the road beyond the sewage treatment plant and follow the signed route across a section of immense **Tuolumne Meadows** for 0.4 mile to the spur road to **Soda Springs**. Turn right and follow the road, or the use path that borders its south (right) side, for 0.8 mile back to Tioga Road. The outcropping immediately to your left (northeast) is **Lembert Dome,** named for a man who homesteaded and raised

sheep here during the 1880s. (A 1.5-mile popular use trail leads along its west and north sides to the summit.) Cross Tioga Road and head southeast through a meadow to just below the summer permit station.

A compromise between the scenic, congested dogleg route along the JMT and the shorter, less populated, but less interesting, southern bypass through woods, is to follow Tioga Road past the stores to the campground entrance and then head south to the intersection with the woodsy detour. To make this shortcut, turn right just beyond the stone information building and follow the paved road to the corner of the camp area, keeping left at all forks so there's never a road between you and the Lyell Fork of the Tuolumne River. At the trail sign leave the road. After several yards veer left so you're on a wide path and traveling parallel to the river. After a short distance come to a stream and the junction of the southerly bypass. See Section B for a description of the route from here east to the JMT.

Tuolumne Meadows from Lembert Dome

TUOLUMNE MEADOWS TO DEVILS POSTPILE

As noted already, the Sierra Nevada supports a wonderful coexistence of the grand and the exquisite. Two superb examples of this juxtaposition are the broad valley of the Lyell Fork of the Tuolumne River, extending for nine miles east and south of Tuolumne Meadows, and Island Pass. The features of the massive valley are softened by the meandering flow and the lush grass — rich green turning to mellow golden as fall approaches. The many fine-boned deer that tread delicately through the valley further enhance the ambience. And there's not a more picture-perfect setting in the High Sierra than that from Island Pass, with dainty tarns and deep grass in the foreground, a snow-splashed, rugged Banner Peak behind, and an expanse of blue sky overhead.

Side Trips. Possible digressions include a short trip to upper and lower Marie Lakes on the south side of Donohue Pass, an easy and enjoyable cross-country excursion from Thousand Island Lake north to Weber Lake, a loop past Iceberg, Cecile, and Minaret lakes or a longer loop to Beck Lakes. The last has merit, of course, but doesn't advance you very far along the JMT.

Exits. Devils Postpile and adjacent Reds Meadow Resort near the 56-mile point are the last places along the JMT where you'll be able to exit directly to a road. From the end of June through Labor Day, shuttle buses run between the parking lot for Mammoth Ski Area on the east side of the Sierra and Devils Postpile, Reds Meadow, and other points. Unless you have a car-camping permit, are an overnight guest of the resort, are carrying eleven or more people, or have nonambulatory persons in your vehicle you cannot drive a private auto west of Minaret Summit between 7:00 A.M. and 8:00 P.M. Shuttle buses in the past have left at frequent intervals from around 8:30 A.M. to 9:30 P.M. However, if you plan to exit or enter here you probably will want to write the Mammoth Visitors Center, Box 148, Mammoth Lakes, California 93546 for a precise schedule and more information on the shuttle system.

You also have the option of exiting along trails from the 40.3-mile point at the Forks of Rush Creek or, 2.8 miles farther along, from Thousand Island Lake, to Silver Lake on the June Lakes Loop road off U.S. 395. A variation is to take the exit trail from Thousand Island Lake but after about two miles turn south and traverse to Agnew Meadows, one of the stops for the Reds Meadow-Devils Postpile shuttle. All aspects considered, the preferable exit is from 48.3 miles at Shadow Lake to Agnew Meadows.

Donohue Pass on the southeastern boundary of Yosemite National Park is the first big crest along the JMT. In relation to some you'll be crossing it's not very demanding, but it certainly is high enough that you should position yourself to cross it early in the day.

Camping Restrictions. Since you're within Yosemite National Park until you reach Donohue Pass, remember that campfires aren't permitted above 9,600 feet — which would be between 33.9 and 37.0 miles. No camping or fires

12

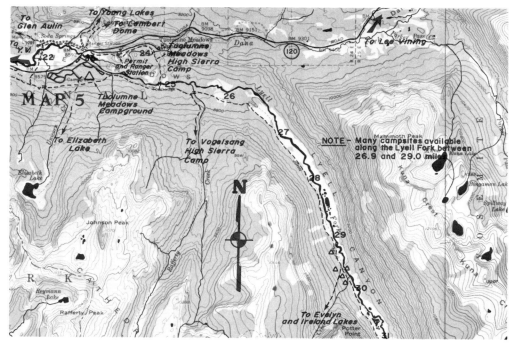

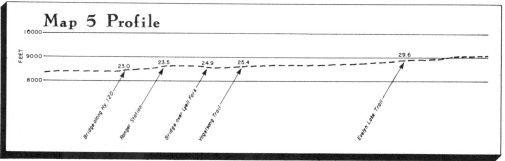

Map 5 Profile

are allowed within one-quarter mile of
the outlets of Thousand Island and
Garnet lakes. At Shadow Lake no
camping or campfires are permitted
along the north shore, and no campfires are allowed along Shadow Creek
from the Shadow Lake inlet to the JMT
junction.

A reminder: Bears are a problem
along all of the JMT in Yosemite National Park, and their unwelcome pres-
ence also is frequently endured at
Thousand Island Lake.

After traveling just below (south of)
the Tuolumne Meadows permit station
and parking lot, the JMT parallels a
road and passes a ranger station. One-
half mile farther, walk below another
large parking area and keep right as
indicated by a big wooden sign. Travel
near the **Dana Fork of the Tuolumne
River** for about 0.1 mile and pass a
50-yard-long side path to a swimming
hole at the base of a cascade. Another
150 yards farther, at the north end of a
bridge over the Dana Fork, is a sign
marking a side trail to Tuolumne
Meadows Lodge. Cross the span and

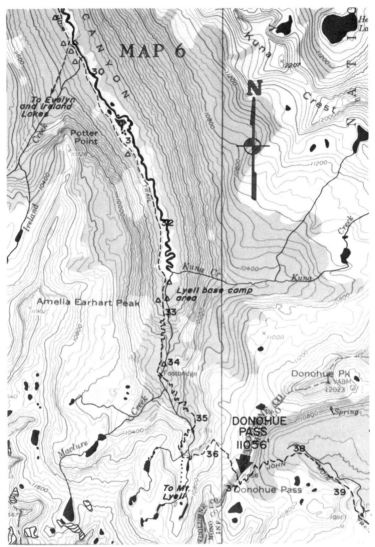

MAP 6

CANYON

To Evelyn
and Ireland
Lakes

Potter
Point

Ireland Creek

Kuna Crest

Amelia Earhart Peak

Kuna Cr.

Kuna

Lyell base camp
area

Footbridge

Maclure Creek

DONOHUE
PASS
11056'

Donohue PK

Spring

To Mt.
Lyell

Donohue Pass

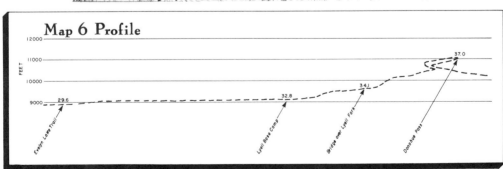

Map 6 Profile

12000

11000

10000

9000

FEET

29.6
Evelyn Lake Trail

32.8
Lyell Base Camp

34.1
Bridge over Lyell Fork

37.0
Donohue Pass

continue south, as indicated by a sign pointing to Donohue Pass. Climb through woods and over a hump, cross the two-part span over the **Lyell Fork of the Tuolumne River,** and continue south a short distance to the junction of the trail from the campground. Beyond this junction, except for the mile south of Devils Postpile, the remaining 182.6 miles of the JMT are uncomplicated.

If you want to follow the trail that skirts the south edge of Tuolumne Meadows, keep right (east) at the junction at 21.5 miles (see Section A). After a short distance cross Budd Creek on a bridge and mostly contour through woods of small trees for 1.2 miles to the junction of the 2.3-mile-long trail to Elizabeth Lake. Keep straight and walk through a deeper forest for 0.5 mile to a stream and the junction of the trail from the southeast end of the campground (also see Section A for a de-

scription of this bypass). Splash across the small flow and two more branches, then walk parallel to the river for 0.7 mile to the junction with the JMT and keep right.

Walk through woods and grassy clearings at a gradual grade. Pass an area of granite slabs and glacial erratics and climb slightly to the junction of a trail to Vogelsang at 25.4 miles. Keep left, and a short distance farther make an easy ford of **Rafferty Creek.** Although grades along the JMT are never steep, neither are they level for a very long distance. The route up Lyell Fork is the one exception, so savor it. Campsites are abundant all along the valley. Just be sure to camp in the woods — not in grassy areas — and at least 100 feet from the river and any side streams.

Eventually you'll be able to glimpse

Area just south of Donohue Pass

the area around Donohue Pass beyond the head of the valley. The sharp peak to your right is **Potter Point**. During the walk along the valley floor stay near Lyell Fork, and farther on at 29.6 miles keep left at the junction of the trail to Evelyn Lake. (If you had opted to detour through Vogelsang, this is the point where you would have rejoined the JMT. You could have met the JMT 4.2 miles back at the junction of the other trail to Vogelsang, but that route is a bit less scenic and you would have lost unnecessary distance had you taken it.)

After a short distance, ford **Ireland Creek** and continue through clearings and fingers of trees, usually traveling close to the river. As you progress you'll have your first good view of Mt. Lyell to the south and, farther on, the end of the valley floor. The voluminous cascade surging down the east wall is Kuna Creek.

Beyond the last campsite at the south end of the valley the smooth tread and level grade cease as you begin to climb. Cross several side streams and an area of avalanche debris that supports a few stunted aspen. Considerably farther along the JMT you'll see many fine specimens of these potentially exquisite trees in the Mono Creek area. As you climb higher you'll be able to gaze down over the oxbow-laced north end of the Lyell Fork valley. Continue switchbacking up through woods to a basin, descend gradually, and 1.3 miles from the valley floor come to a camp area — the last large sheltered place before the Forks of Rush Creek at 40.3 miles.

Cross Lyell Fork on a bridge and resume climbing, crossing a side stream, to a second basin that is considerably more alpine in appearance. Follow the stream through increasingly attractive terrain to an unnamed lake. Cross on logs at the outlet end and climb to a higher basin. Cross a stream here, pass the standard climbers' cross-country

route to Mt. Lyell, and wind up above more lakes to yet another tarn. Continue up treeless slopes to 11,056-foot **Donohue Pass** and a grand view of a large portion of the Minarets Wilderness and east to the desert. The sharp spire on the southern horizon is 12,945-foot Banner Peak.

Wind down through a vast rocky basin, where the trail is sometimes faint and the ground boggy, to a stream crossing. Just beyond it is the junction of the 1.9-mile spur to Marie Lakes that lie directly below the east face of Mt. Lyell.

The trail to Marie Lakes climbs through a small meadow and, 0.5 mile from the JMT, comes to a basin filled with many tarns. Since the few campsites at the lower lake are exposed, this basin would be the preferable place to stay overnight. Switchback steeply up a granite ridge to an overlook about fifty feet above the lower lake and then descend to a small peninsula on the northern shore. The somewhat obscure trail to the upper lake climbs along the granite slopes to the west of the lower lake.

The JMT winds down in switchbacks for 0.2 mile to the marshy **Forks of Rush Creek** and the junction with the trail to Silver Lake, the first exit (or entry) point since Tuolumne Meadows.

This 9.4-mile exit route, involving 420 feet of uphill, traverses above immense Waugh, Gem, and Agnew lakes and then winds down the considerably more arid east side of the Sierra to a small resort at Silver Lake.

Ford the Forks of Rush Creek and begin the gradual, relatively straight forward, 1.3-mile climb through scattered trees to lush, pond-dotted, 10,200-foot **Island Pass** and its exquisite views. Walk on the level through a landscape of grass, scattered rocks, and trees, with perpetual views of Banner Peak and beyond it the barely visible summit wall of Mt. Ritter.

Leave the pass and begin descending. The scene between Island Pass and Garnet Lake is the quintessence of the Sierra: Far-ranging views that encom-

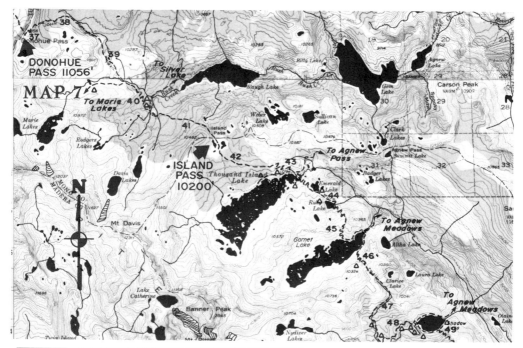

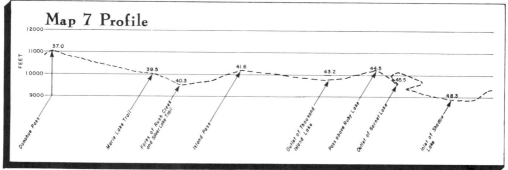

pass expanses of granite slopes, high peaks, huge shimmering blue lakes, enough vegetation to add softness and accents of green, and, most likely, splashes of color from scattered clusters of wild flowers. Where a blocked path heads right, keep left, and after several yards have your first glimpse of Thousand Island Lake. Farther on you'll be able to see the spires of the Minarets and far to the south the peaks around Silver Pass. Cross a few small side streams. Where you traverse a convex slope you can look over the en-

tire expanse of aptly named Thousand Island Lake and also ahead to Emerald Lake and the small basin that holds Ruby Lake. Cross two larger side streams and drop, in two sets of switchbacks, to the junction of the trail to Agnew Pass.

This exit route climbs for 1.4 miles to a junction at the lovely Clark Lakes. From here you can continue up a bit more and then descend to the junction with the trail from Gem and Waugh lakes at the northeast end of Agnew Lake and, as noted earlier, switchback down to Silver Lake on the June Lake Loop road off U.S. 395.

Or you can head southeast from Clark Lakes along the High Trail to Agnew Meadows, located a short distance from the road to Devils Postpile. As noted earlier, the shuttle bus stops at Agnew Meadows. This route traverses high on the sparsely wooded east wall of the deep valley holding the Middle Fork of the San Joaquin River, and you can look across the chasm to Gem and Shadow lakes. Although this High Trail is spectacularly scenic, if you take it you will miss the equally fine country between Thousand Island and Shadow lakes.

Keep right, walk near the shore of **Thousand Island Lake** and cross the outlet on a pole bridge. Remember that no camping or campfires are allowed within one-quarter mile of the outlet. Wind up in a few switchbacks, cross a side stream, and contour above **Emerald Lake.** Make one switchback, again walk on the level, and then travel just inches from the shore of **Ruby Lake.** Make an easy crossing of the outlet and climb in eight switchbacks to a crest. Begin descending, and in a short distance have your first view of massive Garnet Lake, almost the twin of Thousand Island Lake. For the next 1.5 miles you'll again have unobstructed views of Banner Peak and Mt. Ritter. Continue down in a circuitous series of traverses, switchbacks, and windings to the outlet creek. As mentioned earlier, no camping or campfires are permitted within a quarter-mile of **Garnet Lake's outlet.**

The unsigned trail that heads northeast just after the crossing descends to the River Trail, a low-level route between the exit trail from Thousand Island Lake and the one from Shadow Lake. This route is not as scenic as the High Trail or the exit from Shadow Lake.

Cross the outlet on a bridge and travel near the shoreline. Obtain drinking water from either of two adjacent streams, as the next flow you'll encounter is repeatedly crossed by the trail. Begin the inevitable climb (in eighteen switchbacks) to the next crest.

Switchback briefly down the rocky slope to a small meadow, walk to its far end, and then descend along a wee rocky canyon, making three crossings of the small creek that flows down its center. The Minarets can be seen from here. As you lose elevation, enter woods that are the densest since the Forks of Rush Creek. Wind downhill, crossing two small side streams, and at 47.3 miles come above campsites beside a moderately large creek. Veer left, parallel the stream, and then traverse along a more open slope above a meadow area to the junction of the trail with Lake Ediza.

You could make a 9.5-mile (with 1,300 feet of uphill) side loop from here by continuing beyond Lake Ediza and Iceberg Lake to Cecile Lake, then negotiating a bit of cross-country near the west end of a rock band to Minaret Lake, and from it following a trail back to the JMT. The lure of this excursion, in addition to the fine alpine scenery, is that you'd be traveling as close to the Minarets as a trail will take you. No camping is allowed on the south side of Lake Ediza, no campfires are permitted in the watersheds of Lake Ediza or Minaret Lake, and no campfires are legal between the two lakes.

The JMT continues through rocky terrain and soon travels above voluminous **Shadow Creek.** Campsites are abundant between the Lake Ediza junction and Shadow Lake. They are reasonably private, except for the very large one a short distance north of the junction of the exit trail to Agnew Meadows at the west end of Shadow Lake.

This exit route travels along the north shore, winds down the face of the valley, crosses the Middle Fork of the San Joaquin, and then climbs for a modest 400 feet to Agnew Meadows.

Remember that camping and fires are not permitted along the north shore of Shadow Lake, and no campfires are allowed along Shadow Creek from the Shadow Lake inlet to the JMT junction.

Cross the inlet creek on a bridge and

Banner Peak from above Garnet Lake

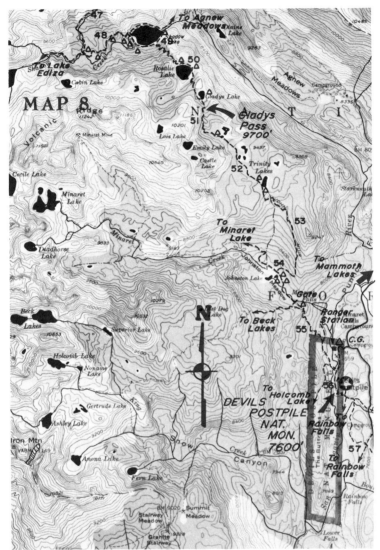

MAP 8

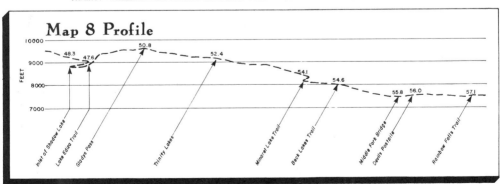

Map 8 Profile

walk in woods near the south shore of **Shadow Lake.** A use path skirts the southeast side if you want to follow it to the outlet end. Begin climbing in many short switchbacks. At the last one, veer left and scramble up over rocks for a view of Shadow Lake and a last good look at Banner, Ritter, and other peaks to the north. Continue uphill for another 100 feet to a crest where you can look down onto **Rosalie Lake.**

Descent briefly, walk around the east side, cross the outlet near a campsite, and climb in a few switchbacks to small **Gladys Lake.** (For a view of Mammoth Mountain and a bird's-eye look into the canyon holding the Middle Fork of the San Joaquin River, leave the trail at the north end of the lake and walk several hundred yards to the rim.) Climb briefly along the JMT, through terrain that may be boggy, to 9,700-foot **Gladys Pass** — even less awesome than Cathedral Pass, which you crossed at 17.3 miles.

The JMT is downhill for the next 5.2 miles to Devils Postpile. For about a mile you'll be traveling through a pleasing transition zone of open woods, grassy pockets, occasional rock outcroppings, streams, and ponds. Although it is near the trail, the largest and lowest of the Trinity Lakes is obscure and easy to miss. About 0.2 mile beyond, it begins descending more noticeably. By this point you've entered dense woods — at least by High Sierra standards — and will be hiking through them for the next 18.0 miles. Well, not precisely the same woods, as the species will be changing. After all, the Sierra *never* is boring or repetitive.

Switchback down, crossing three side streams, and level off just before coming to the junction of the trail to Minaret Lake, 5.0 miles to the west and 1,700 feet higher. (If you made the side loop past Lake Ediza and Iceberg and Cecile lakes you'd rejoin the JMT here.) Turn left, soon pass **Johnston Lake,**

and about 0.2 mile farther come to the ford of **Minaret Creek.** Other than the Forks of Rush Creek, this is the only crossing so far that is a bother — that is, you have to perform one of those rituals described in the main introduction if you want to keep your footwear dry. Later in the season, if there haven't been prolonged storms, you can ford here with no problem. However, if the flow is heavy you may want to head upstream fifty yards or so, where the stream is thigh deep but considerably less rambunctious. From the ford it is 150 yards to the junction of the trail to Beck Lakes.

This 5.0-mile-long trail gains 1,800 feet in elevation as it rises through woods and lush meadows to timberline. The best camping is at the inlet end of Superior Lake, situated about 0.8 mile below the first of the Beck Lakes. You could make a side loop by descending south from the Beck Lakes Trail to Summit Meadow and then heading northeast back to the JMT. Although a scenic, less frequented route, this digression is roundabout and travels perpendicular, not parallel, to the main route.

Keep left again and wind downhill. Pass the sign marking the boundary of **Devils Postpile National Monument,** keep straight at a junction of the short spur to Minaret Falls, and cross two side streams. You can look across a meadow to the parking area for the Postpile. Except for the section through Tuolumne Meadows, this is the only stretch of the JMT where you're not at least a day's hike away from cars. Come to the junction of the trail to Summit Meadow and other points, keep left and 100 feet farther cross the bridge over the **Middle Fork of the San Joaquin River.** (If you're exiting at Devils Postpile or want to visit the ranger station, turn left here and walk north for 0.1 mile.) To continue along the JMT or to visit the facilities at Reds Meadow, keep right after you cross the span.

21

DEVILS POSTPILE TO MONO CREEK

The JMT travels through woods for the initial fourteen miles south of Devils Postpile, but this is no impenetrable forest, as peaks far to the north and south are frequently visible. Besides, this stretch affords a chance to whet your appetite for the timberline setting of Purple and Virginia lakes and, farther on, the expansive landscape that flanks Silver Pass.

Although most people think of the wonderful, light grey granite when they consider the composition of the Sierra, in fact many rocks form the range. No area, anywhere, has a simple geologic history, and the Sierra Nevada is, most definitely, no exception. One contributor to the present configuration was volcanic activity, and the JMT in the region of Devils Postpile is lined with particularly fine examples of this fiery past. There are the postpiles themselves — a wall of hexagonal columns, some up to sixty feet high. If you make the little side loop over the top of the Postpile, you'll see where glacial action has polished the ends of the columns as smooth as an elegant floor. As noted earlier, glaciers were important shapers of the Sierra landscape. Mammoth Mountain nearby to the east was once an active volcano, and Red Cones, which you pass between at 60.0 miles, are, as the name implies, cinder cones. The hot springs at Reds Meadow and elsewhere indicate that future volcanic activity is still a possibility.

Exits. Along this section you can exit east to the Mammoth Lakes area on the Deer Lakes Trail at 62.9 miles, the Duck Pass Trail at 68.4 miles, over McGee Pass from Tully Hole at 74.1 miles, or Mono Pass at 84.3 miles. You'll also have your first opportunity to exit to the west, either over Goodale Pass at 77.9 miles or at the 85.8-mile point. Both of these exits eventually merge and end at Edison Lake. They involve little elevation gain.

Camping Restrictions. Beyond the usual regulations there are no camping restrictions except at Pocket Meadow at 83.0 miles, where overnight stays aren't permitted.

After crossing the span over the Middle Fork of the San Joaquin, head south and jostle with the hordes attracted by the Devils Postpile. This should be your last area of congestion until you reach the last eight miles down the east side of Whitney Portal. About 150 yards from the bridge come to a sign marking the side loop to the top of the Postpile. It soon rejoins the JMT, but staying on the lower route gives you a better look at the columns themselves. Beyond the point where the side loop rejoins, descend slightly to the junction of the route to Rainbow Falls, 1.5 miles away, and the Fish Creek Trail. (You could follow this latter route and rejoin the JMT at 70.3 or 75.6 miles, but it has no features that make it preferable to the JMT.)

Keep left for 150 yards and come to a stream crossing. Definitely don't drink the water, as it flows through an area populated with people and stock. The next mile of trail is chaotic — the most difficult to find along the entire JMT. A short distance beyond the slow-moving stream keep right, unless you want to visit the bathhouse. At an unsigned junction farther on, keep right again. After a couple of hundred feet keep right a third time to continue on the JMT — or turn left to reach Reds Meadow Resort. Travel with slight ups and downs along a small crest and, at an unsigned cross trail, turn left onto it and climb slightly to a wide trail. Cross it, as indicated by a sign, continue uphill, and cross two more perpendicular routes. You're finally out of the maze and should have no further trouble staying on the JMT.

Climb through woods at a mostly

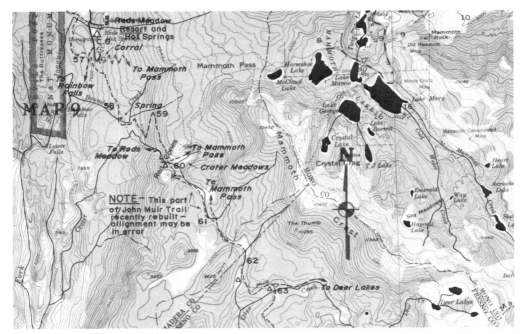

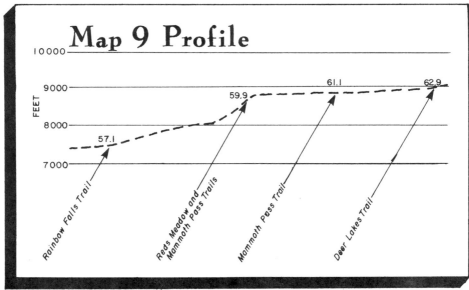

gradual grade along a soft, granular tread, crossing several small side streams. The source of the spring at 58.2 miles is a bizarre-looking pool several yards off the trail on your left. Make the first of three irregularly spaced switchbacks, and as you climb higher you'll have views down into Fish Creek Valley and north to the Minarets, Banner, Ritter, and beyond to the area just south of Donohue Pass. Farther on you can see the two volcanic mounds of Red Cones.

Just before crossing a stream at the base of **Red Cones** an unsigned trail heads east (left) to Reds Meadow and Mammoth Pass. On the other side of the stream, at a campsite, another unmarked route heads west and then north to the Reds Meadow-Devils Postpile area. After a brief level stretch, resume climbing. You'll be able to see the top of the aerial tramway on the summit of Mammoth Mountain and have another view to the north.

Travel near a stream through more open terrain and, about 1.0 mile from Red Cones, keep right at the junction of another trail to Mammoth Pass and Reds Meadow. This route was the former alignment of the JMT. Walk at an almost level grade, curve through a meadow area with a pumice surface, then parallel a stream through a grassy swale. Cross the flow and descend gradually to a sign identifying the Deer Creek Crossing.

A possibly unsigned trail heads east for 2.5 miles along Deer Creek to Deer Lakes. From there you can hike another 6.0 miles to a parking area 3.5 miles from the busy community of Mammoth Lakes. The total distance and elevation gain from the JMT to the exit trailhead is 8.5 miles and 2,100 feet. The trip from Deer Lakes is expansively scenic, and several miles of it are along the broad, treeless spine of Mam-

The Minarets from near Red Cones

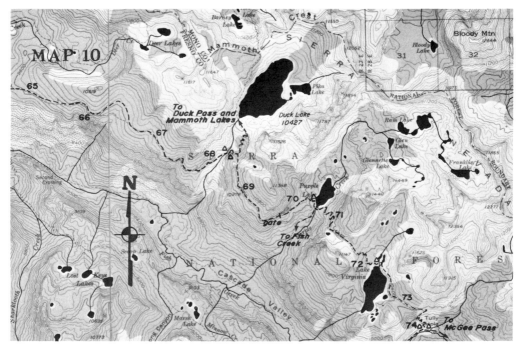

MAP 10

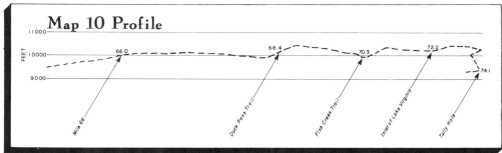

Map 10 Profile

moth Crest. Be sure to obtain adequate drinking water at Deer Lakes, as you'll cross no streams the rest of the way.

Pass a campsite and cross **Deer Creek.** Begin a moderate climb through woods, and traverse high along the north wall of huge Fish Creek Valley. Farther on you'll have views to the south. Travel at a fairly level grade in and out of two side canyons, then begin descending into the large side valley holding Duck Creek. At an open area at 68.1 miles you can see across the clearing to good campsites on the other side of the stream. The trail crosses **Duck**

Creek and winds uphill for 0.2 mile to the junction of the trail to Duck Lake and Pass.

Duck Lake is one of the largest in the High Sierra accessible only by trail. This exit to the Mammoth Lakes area passes lakes and travels through lush alpine terrain, in contrast to the stark country bordering the Deer Lakes Trail along Mammoth Crest. The distance from the JMT to the Duck Lake trailhead is 6.0 miles, with 700 feet of uphill. The parking area is 5.0 miles from Mammoth Lakes.

Turn right and wind uphill along the slope dotted with trees and boulders. One-third mile from the Duck Lake junction begin contouring above Cascade Valley. Farther on you'll be able to see ahead to Goodale and Silver passes — you'll be crossing the latter. At 69.5 miles curve into the side canyon holding Purple Creek and descend along the north wall. About 0.3 mile before **Purple Lake** begin winding down through deeper woods and come to the grassy southwestern shore. To reach campsites, veer left from the trail and contour to the north for a few hundred feet. Continue along the JMT to the junction of a trail down to Fish Creek, keep left, and cross the bridge over the outlet.

Climb in switchbacks through a more open timberline setting and come to a narrow, rocky canyon. Traverse along its northeast wall to a crest. Soon after you begin descending the other side you will have a glimpse of **Virginia Lake**. Continue down to the grassy area at its north end, cross the inlet creek, and then travel above the east shore along a rocky slope. Walk on the level across more pumice, then begin descending. Very soon you will be able to peer down into Tully Hole, as you continue dropping in many switchbacks to its grassy floor. Pass a campsite on your left in a grove of tall trees, 100 feet farther cross a small side stream, and in about 100 yards come to the junction of the exit trail over 11,950-foot McGee Pass.

The exit over this route to the trailhead at the end of McGee Creek Road 4.0 miles from U.S. 395 involves 2,380 feet of uphill, all gained during the climb from Tully Hole to McGee Pass. The scenery along this exit includes many lakes and lush grassy areas. However, early in the season or after prolonged stormy weather, the ford of McGee Creek 2.6 miles from the east end of the exit could be a bit of a problem. In the past there has been a good crossing about 0.2 mile downstream, although this can change from year to year.

Keep straight and travel downhill beside noisy **Fish Creek** for about 1.0 mile, switchback once, and then cross the stream on a big bridge. Pass a good camp area off the right side of the trail, and 100 yards farther reach the junction of the trail down Fish Creek Valley.

Keep left, climb in many switchbacks, and then continue winding up over the wooded and rocky terrain. Travel beside a stream, pass a campsite, the last sheltered one on the north side of Silver Pass, and cross the flow. After 150 yards recross the stream on a bridge at the edge of a pretty, little meadow. Wind up through increasingly open terrain to a basin, continue climbing to a second one, and switchback up to timberline and the bowl that holds **Squaw Lake** (shown as Helen Lake on old topo maps). Cross the outlet and have another look back to Banner and Ritter. Climb for 0.5 mile to a crest and continue up along it for another 150 yards to the junction of the trail over Goodale Pass.

This trail to Edison Lake, the first exit to the west, is 11.5 miles with 750 feet of uphill. However, you can reach the same roadhead with about the same amount of climbing and distance by continuing along the JMT to a junction about 1.0 mile east of the north end of Edison Lake. Both routes have their virtues, and one can't be recommended over the other.

Keep left, and after a few hundred yards pass near the north side of **Chief Lake** (shown as Warrior Lake on old topo maps). Resume winding uphill, soon rise above timberline, pass near **Warrior Lake** (formerly Bobs Lake) and continue climbing to 10,900-foot **Silver Pass** on the boundary between the Inyo and Sierra national forests. The spires to the southeast are the Seven Gables.

Switchback down among rounded rock outcroppings, pass a tarn, and continue descending to the flat basin holding grass-rimmed **Silver Pass Lake**. Soon come to the first woods and resume descending. Cross **Silver Pass Creek** and continue down through denser woods to a second stream. Travel through an attractive meadowy

Lake Virginia

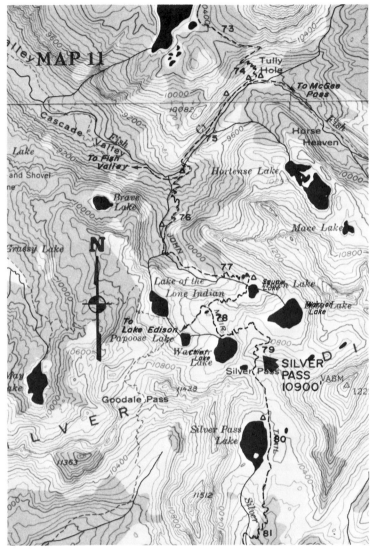

MAP 11

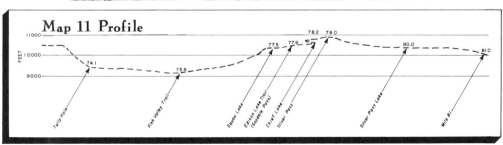

Map 11 Profile

Trail sign near Crater Meadow

swale to near a brushy clearing at 82.3 miles. Beyond it begin winding steeply downhill in short, steep switchbacks to the second ford of Silver Pass Creek. Continue down to the log crossing of the **North Fork of Mono Creek** and in a few hundred feet meet the trail to Mott Lake.

You could make an extremely scenic loop by climbing up to Mott Lake, following a moderately easy cross-country route up to Rosey Finch Lake, continuing up to a crest, and from there descending to Grinnel and Laurel lakes, then following the Mono Pass Trail back to the JMT. This circuit would be 12.0 miles with a total elevation gain of 2,200 feet. This fine loop rejoins the JMT just 1.5 miles south of the Mott Lake junction.

Continue downhill, pass bushy **Pocket Meadow**, where camping is not allowed, travel beside the North Fork as it flows pleasantly over granite slabs, then wind down over rocky terrain and past some aspen trees to the junction of the

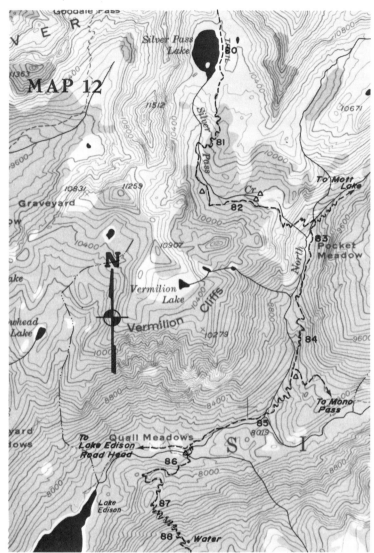

MAP 12

Goodale Pass

Silver Pass
Lake

80

81

Silver Pass

11512

11363

Cr

82

To Mott
Lake

North

83
Pocket
Meadow

Graveyard

10831

11259

10907

N

Vermilion
Lake

Vermilion

Cliffs

10279

84

To Mono
Pass

Lake

85

To
Lake Edison
Road Head

Quail Meadows

S

86

Lake
Edison

87

88   Water

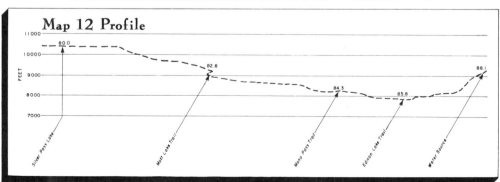

Map 12 Profile

11000

80.0

10000

82.8

FEET

9000

88.1

84.3

85.8

8000

7000

Silver Pass Lake

Mott Lake Trail

Mono Pass Trail

Edison Lake Trail

Water Source

Crater Creek

trail over the southern Mono Pass. The northern pass is also on the Sierra crest but is on the eastern boundary of Yosemite National Park. (If you made the Mott-Laurel Lake side loop you'd be coming out here.)

The exit over Mono Pass from the JMT to the Rock Creek roadhead 11.0 miles from U.S. 395 is 14.5 miles with 3,800 feet of uphill. This is an exceptionally scenic way out, with the possibility of side trips into Second, Third and Fourth Recesses as well as to Pioneer Basin.

Keep right and eventually begin descending more moderately along a smoother tread. Ford the North Fork of Mono Creek and hike gradually downhill through deep woods for 0.8 mile to the junction of the 7.0-mile, mostly level exit trail along the north shore of Edison Lake. Campsites are available a short distance along this exit route.

MONO CREEK TO PIUTE CREEK

If you're taking time for side trips from the JMT, the upper Bear Creek drainage definitely is a prime area to visit. Especially recommended are excursions to Lake Italy and Italy Pass and to the Seven Gables Lakes, leaving the JMT at 94.9 and 96.2 miles, respectively. Both these explorations can be done as day hikes from a base camp. Also highly recommended is a side loop that leaves the JMT at 97.6 miles, passes Sandpiper Lake, and rejoins the main route at Marie Lake after a section of easy cross-country travel.

Selden Pass, just barely at timberline, is the last easy one you'll encounter along the JMT. Since water and campsites are plentiful between 92.8 miles and Sally Keyes Lakes on the south side of Selden Pass at 102.0 miles, you have the luxury of a flexible schedule.

Exits. You can exit east over Italy Pass or over the rolling, broad expanse of Piute Pass from the 109.2-mile point. Routes to the west leave the JMT at 92.8, 105.9, and 107.4 miles. The first follows Bear Creek to a road near Mono Hot Springs Resort, and the second and third end at Florence Lake.

Camping Restrictions. No special camping restrictions are in effect along this section.

Turn left and cross **Mono Creek** on a large bridge. After a wee climb and descent, head west for about 0.5 mile, cross a stream, and resume traveling south through an area of hearty aspen — exquisite deciduous trees that are even more exceptional in fall when their leaves turn a bright yellow. Cross two side streams, begin winding uphill, and then pass through a lush basin of even grander aspen. Resume climbing in many short switchbacks through woods composed of tall conifers and minimal ground cover. At one of the switchbacks you are near a stream that is reached by an obvious side path. This creek is the last water for more than three miles.

Continue switchbacking and then climb in less-defined turns before enjoying a 1.4 mile respite of a nearly level traverse across the nose of 9,980-foot **Bear Ridge.** At 91.0 miles begin winding downhill through aspen, junipers, and wild flowers. After about 0.5 mile of descent begin a traverse to the southeast, cross two side streams, and come to the junction of the Bear Creek Trail. **Kip Camp** between the JMT and the Bear Creek Trail is a large area and for that reason is not especially desirable unless you happen to be there when it's sparsely populated. Many other sites are available as you travel beside Bear Creek.

The 8.0-mile exit (with about 350 feet of uphill) along the Bear Creek Trail meets the road to Edison Lake one mile north of the spur to the resort at Mono Hot Springs. If you take this route, watch for rattlesnakes along the last two miles.

Turn left and walk beside or very near wide **Bear Creek** over terrain covered with granite outcroppings and good-sized conifers, passing many campsites, for 2.0 miles to a junction on your left marked by a sign reading *Trail.* This is the route up Hilgard Canyon to Lake Italy, the first of several

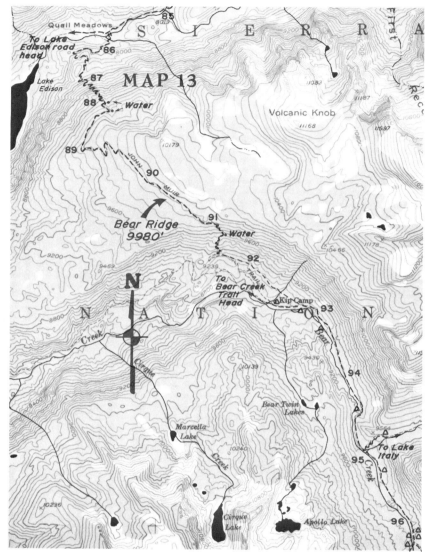

Quail Meadows

To Lake
Edison road
head

Lake
Edison

MAP 13

SIERRA

Volcanic Knob

Water

JOHN MUIR

Bear Ridge
9980'

Water

To Bear Creek
Trail Head

Kip Camp

N

Creek

Cirque

Bear Twin
Lakes

Marcella
Lake

To Lake
Italy

Creek

Cirque
Lake

Apollo Lake

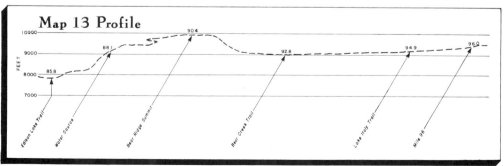

Map 13 Profile

Bear Creek

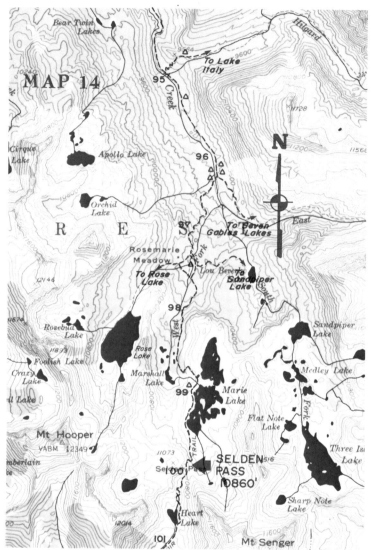

MAP 14

Bear Twin Lakes

To Lake Italy

95

Creek

Hilgard

11728

N

11200

11566

Cirque Lake

Apollo Lake

96

Orchid Lake

R   E   S   To Bench Lakes

Gables

East

Rosemarie Meadow

To Rose Lake

Lou Beverly

Sandpiper Lake

Fork

West

South

12146

98

Rosebud Lake

11574

Sandpiper Lake

11893

Rose Lake

Foolish Lake

Crazy Lake

Marshall Lake

Medley Lake

99

Marie Lake

Fork

Mt Hooper

VABM 12349

11073

Flat Note Lake

Three Isl Lake

11516

Chamberlain

Selden Pass

100

SELDEN PASS 10860'

Sharp Note Lake

Heart Lake

12014

TRAIL

101

11600

Mt Senger

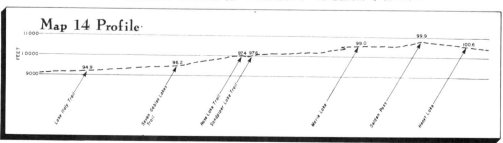

Map 14 Profile

11000

FEET

10000

9000

94.9

96.2

974 976

99.0

99.9

100.6

Lake Italy Trail

Seven Gables Lakes Trail

Rose Lake Trail

Sandpiper Lake Trail

Marie Lake

Selden Pass

Heart Lake

Trail above the South Fork of the San Joaquin River

side trips you can make in the Bear Creek drainage.

The route to Lake Italy, which has the shape of its namesake, gains 1,850 feet in 4.0 miles. From the lake you can continue up another 1,200 feet over Italy Pass, from there descend through lovely Granite Park to the Pine Creek Pass Trail, and follow it down to the Pine Creek roadhead 9.0 miles from U.S. 395. This is only a moderately popular trailhead, so hitching a ride might be a bit of a problem.

Just beyond the Lake Italy trail junction cross two small streams and then come to formidable **Hilgard Creek.** Check upstream for a possible log to scoot or walk across. Continue up at a gradual grade for about 1.2 miles to the edge of a grassy area. You can avoid the Bear Creek ford 0.1 mile ahead (wide and safe but usually too deep to keep feet dry) by turning right and looking for logs across the split stream.

Turn left on the opposite side, pass through a camp area, and rejoin the JMT. If you don't want to deviate from the JMT, head on the level for another 0.1 mile beyond the optional crossing to the junction of the trail to Seven Gables and Vee lakes.

The 3.0-mile, 1,450-foot climb along the East Fork of Bear Creek to the lush, almost treeless basin holding the Seven Gables Lakes is the second of the possible side trips in the Bear Creek area. A mile of easy cross-country travel beyond Seven Gables Lakes will take you to Vee Lake.

Curve right at the junction of the spur to Seven Gables and Vee lakes and almost immediately ford Bear Creek. Wind up through woods with a rocky ground cover, and about 1.1 miles from the ford come to the eastern end of **Rosemarie Meadow**. Cross the **West Fork of Bear Creek** on a pole bridge. A short distance beyond the bridge pass the possibly unsigned trail on your left to Lou Beverly and Sandpiper lakes.

You can make an exquisitely scenic, easy cross-country loop from Sandpiper Lake to Marie Lake where you rejoin the JMT. This side trip is 3.0 miles with a 700-foot climb. Since you gain 650 feet and travel 1.6 miles along the JMT, this digression doesn't involve much extra work or time. Once you've reached Sandpiper Lake, go around its south side and climb moderately toward the north end of the high rock ridge to the west, then follow a use trail across the face of the slope. Continue to the crest of the low ridge that runs in a north-south direction. There you'll be able to look down onto Marie Lake and see the isthmus near its midpoint that is a good place to cross.

Walk along the edge of the meadow for a few hundred yards to the junction, also possibly unsigned, on your right of the 1.0-mile-long trail to Rose Lake. Keep left and begin winding up the slope of boulders, rock slabs, and

Meadow below the Sally Keyes Lakes

37

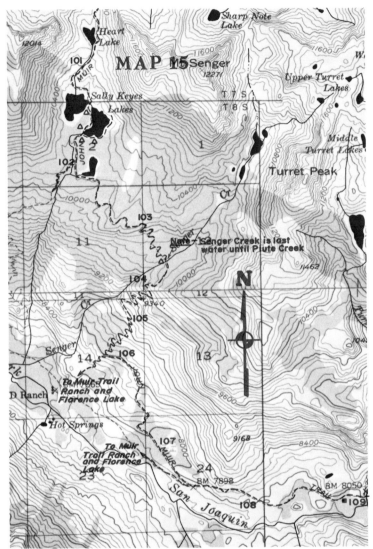

MAP 15

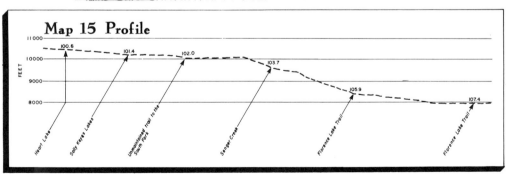

Map 15 Profile

Trail on south side of Selden Pass

scattered trees. Traverse on the level, then climb the last bit of uphill to the edge of the large, almost treeless basin holding complex **Marie Lake.** Walk along the length of the western shore and begin climbing along the head of the basin. As you gain elevation you'll have an unobstructed view over Marie Lake. Make one set of switchbacks and arrive at knobby, rock-dotted, 10,860-foot **Selden Pass.**

Look down the canyon of rocks and trees on the south side of the pass to Heart Lake, then wind down through the defile. Cross the inlet stream twice and travel above **Heart Lake.** Follow the outlet down through a notch, and as you continue descending you'll be able to see below to Sally Keyes Lakes. Cross the outlet from Heart Lake twice, then cross the flow from the upper of the two **Sally Keyes Lakes** (although it's higher by only a few feet), and walk through woods along the western shore of the lower one. Just beyond the crossing of the outlet bear right and walk through a large meadow. Wind down through woods, then climb briefly and traverse. Descend to a small meadow that may hold water early in the season and continue down to the crossing of **Senger Creek,** the last source of water until the crossing of Piute Creek 5.5 miles ahead. This is the longest dry stretch along the JMT, and the aridity is augmented by the south-facing slope farther on, vegetated with pine and manzanita.

Come to a great view of the canyon of the South Fork of the San Joaquin River and soon begin switchbacking down the open, bush-covered slope. Reenter woods and continue descending to the junction of the trail to Florence Lake.

This 10.0-mile, mostly level exit to the west ends at a somewhat less popular trailhead than the one at Edison Lake and the one along the Bear Creek Trail.

Keep left, traverse a lush slope, then travel gradually downhill through a pleasant forest of pine and manzanita to the junction with another trail to Florence Lake that connects in 1.2 miles with the one you could have taken at the 105.9-mile point. Keep straight (left) and follow a gradual uphill grade along a reddish colored rocky slope of widely spaced ponderosa pines. You can hear, but infrequently see, the South Fork of the San Joaquin River roaring along its channel several hundred feet downslope. At 109.2 miles come to the junction of the trail through Hutchinson Meadow and over Piute Pass, the last straightforward exit until the route over Bishop Pass, 25.8 miles and 3,900 feet farther uphill.

Piute Pass is of the broad, grassy, and tarn-dotted rather than rocky-and-narrow school. The trip out is 16.5 miles, with 3,500 feet of uphill, and ends at North Lake. If you exit here and have the inclination, you can make an impressive side trip from about 1.2 miles west of Piute Pass to Desolation Lake. The loop from North Lake over Piute Pass, south along the JMT over Muir Pass, then out to South Lake over Bishop Pass is, justifiably, one of the most popular circuits in the High Sierra.

PIUTE CREEK TO DUSY CREEK

South of Piute Creek the landscape becomes considerably more bold, with peaks and expanses of ridges rising far above timberline and immense basins flanking the big passes. If the northern part of the High Sierra is the Aristocracy, the terrain south of Piute Creek is the Royal Family.

You'll feel like a giant propagating sine wave as you chug up and over the six remaining passes: Muir, Mather, Pinchot, Glen, Forester, and Trail Crest. The first 110 miles of the JMT supposedly has prepared your body and mind for the demands of the second half. It's not that the grades are steeper or their surfaces rougher, but rather that the uphill stretches are considerably more protracted and campsites, overall, are less frequent.

Exits. The only straightforward exit is at the end of this section, along the trail that climbs through lovely Dusy Basin and over Bishop Pass to South Lake. Be forewarned that this is one of the most popular access points on the east side and is often crowded. Parking spaces at the Bishop Pass trailhead are very limited; if you intend to start from here, try to arrive early in the morning, preferably on a weekday. An extremely demanding cross-country exit from Evolution Valley over Lamarck Col to North Lake also is possible, and you can exit west from the 113.5-mile point over a roundabout route up Goddard Canyon, over Hell-For-Sure Pass, and down to Courtright Reservoir.

Since the approach to Muir Pass from the north is a long, gradual climb well above timberline, you'll want to place your camp so that, hopefully, you can get over the crest before thunderstorms develop. Don't be put off by these repeated warnings about thunderstorms. Lightning storms are not a daily occurence in the Sierra, but by planning ahead you can avoid being caught in a place where you'll feel even more vulnerable than the proverbial sitting duck if a storm does occur.

Camping Restrictions. The only special camping restriction along this section of the JMT is that wood fires are not allowed from Evolution Lake to Muir Pass.

Cross the large (and welcome) bridge over **Piute Creek,** veer right, and pass a register and a sign marking the boundary of **Kings Canyon National Park.** Until you reach Trail Crest at 205.6 miles, you'll be traveling through Kings Canyon and then Sequoia national parks for the remaining distance along the JMT. Pass just above a good camp area and walk along an attractive canyon of high, rock walls. Along one stretch travel above the river through a gorge. Enter denser vegetation, including an aspen grove, and cross a side stream. Except for this stretch and a second one farther on in the woods, the trail up the canyon has a rocky surface. Continue paralleling the river as it assumes various guises — wide and shallow, tumbling cascades, and surging flows through narrow gorges. Cross a large bridge across the **South Fork of the San Joaquin.** There are many campsites near the trail between here and the second crossing, 1.2 miles farther along. Travel on the level, occasionally through lush vegetation, cross a broad,

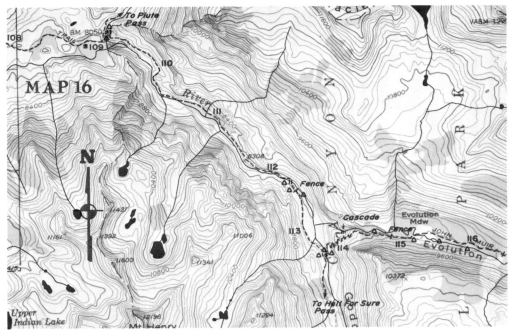

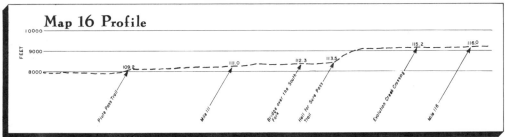

shallow stream, and come to the junction of the exit trail to Courtright Reservoir.

This exit is 23.5 miles with 2,950 feet of uphill, along a route that is a bit obscure and complicated in places — precisely what some people thoroughly enjoy. If you want to follow it, keep right and traverse along the west wall of Goddard Canyon for 5.0 miles to the junction of the Hell-For-Sure Pass Trail. Turn right and climb for 3.0 miles back along the canyon wall, then switchback up to the 11,297-foot pass. From here you'll have a superb view over Red Mountain Basin where there are many good campsites. From the pass, drop into the basin and pass a collection of lakes and tarns. As you continue down, don't follow trails south to Devils Punch-

bowl or north to Rae Lake, or, farther on, to Burnt Corral Meadows. If you intend to exit this way, you should acquire a recreation map of the Sierra National Forest.

Keep left, recross the South Fork of the San Joaquin River on a bridge, walk on the level for 200 yards, and just beyond where you pass a campsite begin winding up a rocky slope on a rough trail. Pass a side path to a view of a cascade and then leave the west-facing slope and curve into the side canyon formed by **Evolution Creek**. Travel beside the ever-changing progression of pools, rapids, and falls. Come to a pole fence, pass a horse crossing, and continue upstream a

South Fork of the San Joaquin River near Goddard Canyon

short distance to a good log crossing. After rejoining the official route, traverse up and away from the stream, pass a campsite on your right at the west end of **Evolution Meadow,** and beyond the clearing resume climbing through woods.

Go through a second pole gate, cross a stream, and continue up to the western edge of **McClure Meadow.** A path heads left to a pit toilet, and fine campsites are available on the right (south) side of the trail. Although camping here is excellent, with a superb view up **Evolution Valley** to the peaks at its head, you need an early start for the push over Muir Pass. Walk by the ranger station above the north side of the trail, continue up along the northern edge of the meadow, and climb gradually in woods, crossing many side streams, to **Colby Meadow.** Cross two more side streams and soon begin wind-

ing uphill, passing a viewpoint with a good view down the valley. The black mass behind the lighter ridge to the west is Emerald Peak.

The evolutionary theme doesn't end with Evolution Valley, Darwin Canyon, and Lamarck Col; the surrounding peaks include Mts. Huxley, Spencer, Wallace, and Haeckel. These names were given by Theodore Solomons, who explored the area in 1895. His first big trip into the Sierra was in 1892, when he took the first photographs of Mt. Ritter. Two years later his group journeyed farther south to the Bear Creek drainage and, among other adventures, made the first ascent of the Seven Gables.

The obscure and unmaintained 4.0-mile route that leaves the JMT at 120.7 miles and climbs through Darwin Canyon to 12,900-foot Lamarck Col is quite a challenge, with its boulder-strewn terrain, but

Hikers crossing Evolution Creek

this cross-country trek is done frequently. From the col a good trail descends for 5.0 miles through impressive terrain to popular North Lake. (Gas stoves only in Darwin Canyon.)

Continue switchbacking up, passing the unmarked trail to Lamarck Col at the last turn. Cross a little side stream, rise above timberline, and wind among the charming setting of grass, rocks, and tarns to **Evolution Lake.** Walk near the lake, climb over a grassy hump, then return to the shore and follow along the length of the eastern side. Cross a little inlet flow and follow near the east side of the outlet from **Sapphire Lake.**

If the crossing just above the south end of Evolution Lake is too deep, you have the option of following along the east side of the stream until you find a ford more to your liking. The JMT travels near the western shore of Sap-

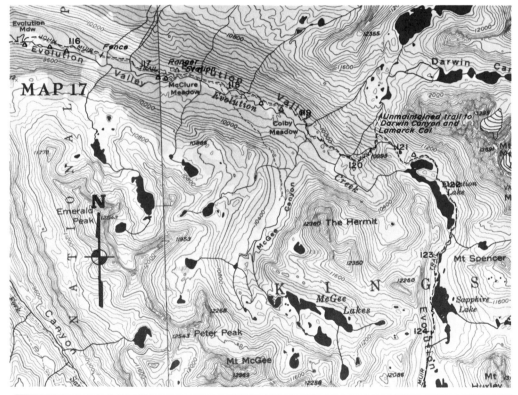

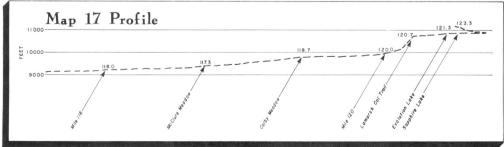

Trail along the South Fork of the San Joaquin River near Goddard Canyon

phire Lake for half its length and then climbs above it. Rise gradually along the mostly rocky trail past an unnamed lake, cross a shallow stream, and come to immense **Wanda Lake.** You'll be able to see Muir Pass and the hut there, as well as southwest to the black hulk of Mt. Goddard.

Skirt the shoreline and begin — gratefully — a gradual climb. Cross a wide, shallow stream between two tarns and continue meandering up over the barren terrain. As you gain eleva-

tion you can look back down over Wanda Lake and Evolution Basin, the most magnificently bleak expanse along the JMT. Early in the season many small streams trickle down the slope, but as summer wanes they become undependable water sources.

When you finally reach 11,955-foot **Muir Pass** you'll want to examine the beehive-shaped shelter there, built in 1929 for $5,900 from funds donated by one individual. Its architecture is almost identical to the structure at the

"Laughing Rock" in Evolution Basin

Keyhole on Longs Peak in Rocky Mountain National Park, Colorado, except that the latter snuggles up to a rock wall on one side. The design is taken from huts found in Brindisi, Italy. As interesting as the building is, and as welcome as it could be in foul weather, don't plan to stay there overnight except in emergencies. Like most shelters, it tends to leak and be dank.

From Muir Pass wind down among several tarns and travel along the southeast shore of **Helen Lake.** All the streams on this side of Muir Pass form the headwaters of the **Middle Fork of the Kings River.** Walk through a rugged, rocky gorge that looks more like it belongs in the desert than in the High Sierra and travel along a wall above an unnamed lake. Descend, cross a slope of many small rivulets, ford the outlet, and continue down in switchbacks through another defile to the first of the stunted trees. Come to a tarn, descend to a large lake, and cross its inlet. Walk along the southern

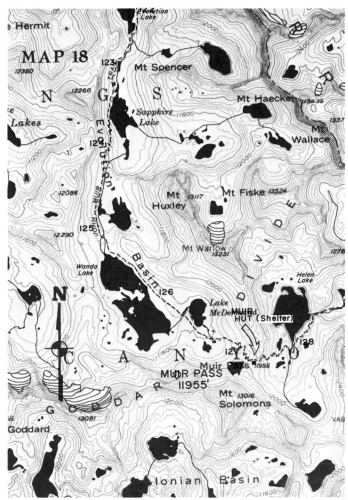

MAP 18

N G S

Mt Spencer

Mt Haeckel

Sapphire
Lake

Mt
Wallace

N

Lakes

Evolution
Basin
Trail

Mt Fiske

Mt
Huxley

Mt Warlow

Wanda
Lake

Basin

126

Helen
Lake

Lake
McDe...Muir Rd
HUT (Shelter)

N

C

A

128

Muir Pass

MUIR PASS
11955'

Mt
Solomons

Goddard

Goddard

Ionian Basin

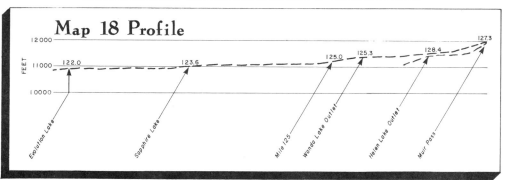

Map 18 Profile

12000

FEET

11000 122.0   123.6   125.0   125.3   128.4   127.3

10000

Evolution Lake   Sapphire Lake   Mile 125   Wanda Lake Outlet   Helen Lake Outlet   Muir Pass

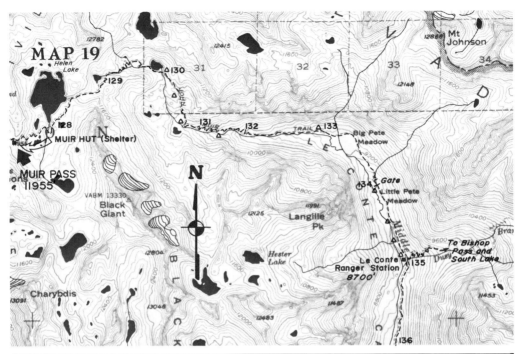

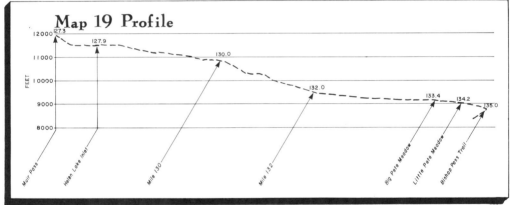

shore, cross the outlet, and wind down a hummocky valley, where good campsites are numerous. If you intend to spend the night in the area, be sure to select a site before you begin the switchbacks at 130.8 miles down the head of very steep **Le Conte Canyon.**

After considerable switchbacking, straighten out and hike parallel to the Middle Fork of the Kings River through denser woods. Cross two small side streams and pass **Big Pete Meadows,** where you have a good view down the remainder of Le Conte Canyon to Devils Crags and beyond. Joseph Le Conte explored the Sierra extensively from the mid-1890s to the early 1900s. While on these trips he made triangulations of peaks from Mt. Ritter south to Mt. Whitney.

Continue traversing down a slope of small conifers and avalanche-bent

Muir Pass and Mt. Solomons

aspen and pass through a gate, where you have a good view of **Little Pete Meadow** and the sheer granite face of Langille Peak looming above it. Cross two adjacent side streams, pass a few small campsites, and follow a smooth trail down a quasi-gorge to the path to the **Le Conte Ranger Station** and, just a few feet farther, the junction of the exit trail over Bishop Pass to South Lake.

The straightforward climb up to the pass is 7.0 miles with 3,300 feet of elevation gain, and the rest of the way to South Lake is all downhill for another 6.0 miles. Most of the first 3.0 miles of uphill is unremitting switchbacks to lovely Dusy Basin. Particularly fine campsites are across Dusy Creek at the west end of the basin, and staying here puts you in a good position to get over Bishop Pass and out to South Lake by early afternoon. No wood fires are permitted between the bridge over Dusy Creek and Bishop Pass.

DUSY CREEK TO THE SOUTH FORK OF THE KINGS RIVER

In one sense this is an uncomplicated section of the JMT. After continuing downhill near the Middle Fork of the Kings River for another 3.7 miles, the route turns sharply east, begins the pull up Palisade Creek valley, passes above Palisade Lakes, makes the final pitch to Mather Pass, then winds di-

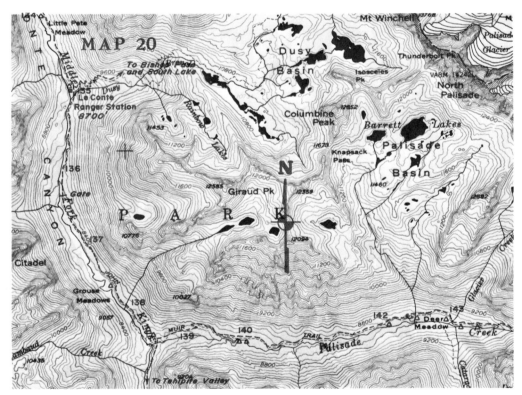

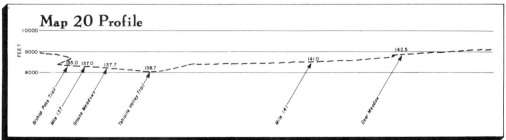

rectly down the other side to the tundra of Upper Basin. Of course this basic cake is frosted with the standard delectable Sierra scenery.

Most of the crowds milling about at the Le Conte Ranger Station and near Dusy Creek are backpackers making the North Lake-South Lake loop over Piute, Muir, and Bishop passes, and, as you continue south, congestion thins very quickly. Barring unfortuitous timing you should encounter the fewest fellow travelers on the JMT between Grouse Meadow (137.7 miles) and Twin Lakes (163.9 miles).

Exits. Two reasons why the JMT isn't as heavily populated between Grouse Meadow and Twin Lakes is that neither access is easy. The exit from 138.7 miles west out through Tehipite Valley is not only long and circuitous, it also is infamous for heat and the abundance of rattlesnakes. The route from the east over Taboose Pass that meets the JMT at its 157.3-mile point is considerably more direct, but the elevation gain of 6,300 feet in the first 9.0 miles is a deterrent for most. Exiting over Taboose Pass is, of course, not so arduous.

Camping Restrictions. No wood fires — gas stoves only — are permitted at Palisade Lakes.

Walk gradually downhill and soon cross a bridge over tumbling **Dusy Creek.** Campsites are plentiful south from the ranger station to a short distance beyond Dusy Creek. Leave the woods and travel through more open terrain above the river. Cross a few side streams and pass through a gate. The stream down the opposite wall comes from Ladder Lake. Pass through an area of avalanche debris, enter attractive, deeper woods, and continue mostly gradually downhill to lush **Grouse Meadows.** This soggy, verdant meadow most likely began as a lake. As sediment from inlet streams filled the lake, grass started to grow. After a

meadow has been formed, and if conditions are favorable, trees begin to establish themselves along the fringes of the open area. Eventually, what was once a lake and then a meadow will become a forest. As you travel along the JMT you'll observe many examples of this inexorable transition.

Pass several camp areas, drop through more open, rocky terrain, and come to another campsite at the end of the descent. Collect your climbing muscles! There's little downhill for 11.4 miles until Mather Pass, although you will have an occasional welcome level stretch. Climb for a few hundred feet to the junction of the exit trail to Cartridge Creek, Simpson Meadow, and Tehipite Valley.

Keep left — don't cross the bridge — and continue uphill through an area of manzanita, pines, a few healthy ferns, and aspen, the last becoming more plentiful farther on. About 1.4 miles from the junction, pass a good campsite on your right. Spaces also are off the trail on the left. Hike at an erratic, but never steep, grade through woods of varying composition, and 2.0 miles from the last one pass another campsite. Enter deeper woods and continue the irregular uphill. Cross three good-sized streams, passing a campsite beyond the third one. Traverse the brushy, open slope near **Deer Meadow** (that you really never see) and reenter the woods. Cross several more side streams, pass the last two sheltered campsites until 4.3 miles south of Mather Pass, and begin climbing through increasingly open terrain.

Begin the many switchbacks up the rocky section of trail known as the **Golden Staircase.** This portion of the JMT was the last segment to be completed along the original alignment. Despite construction problems, it is not as impressive as the name implies. Perhaps it would be somewhere else, but not in the Sierra. However, during the climb you will have views over the

Grouse Meadows

valley you've just passed through, and you will have the minty scent of pennyroyal to perk you up. Wind up into a hidden, convoluted basin — an abrupt but pleasant transition. As you round one corner there is a view north to the Palisade Crest. On the sides of the crest that you can't see are the largest ice masses in California. They're meager in comparison to the glaciers in the Washington Cascades and insignificant by Alaskan standards, but they are glaciers, nonetheless.

Enter a lovely alpine area of grass, rocks, and streams and come to the west end of the lower of two **Palisade Lakes.** Enjoy a brief respite as you walk near the northern shoreline, and then resume climbing. Noisy marmots are numerous here. Farther on you'll have a view ahead to the upper lake and Mather Pass. Traverse high above the upper lake and, just about at its midpoint, pass a campsite on a bench in

a grove of trees on your right. Although this location is reasonably well sheltered considering its proximity to timberline, it is the last one for 5.0 miles, until you reach the other side of Mather Pass at the 155.5-mile point. You'd be in a logistically bad position if you had planned to stay here and the site already was occupied.

One hundred yards beyond the campsite cross a good-sized stream and continue traversing. Drop in one short set of switchbacks, then resume climbing and rise above the last of the trees. The third side stream you cross is the last source of water for 3.0 miles. Climb to a basin and make the final series of switchbacks and traverses along a relatively smooth tread up to 12,100-foot **Mather Pass.** Actually, the trail meets the crest a bit above the pass proper, so you'll have a slight drop at the end. As with any high pass, hopefully the weather will be pleasant so you can

Palisade Crest from the top of the Golden Staircase

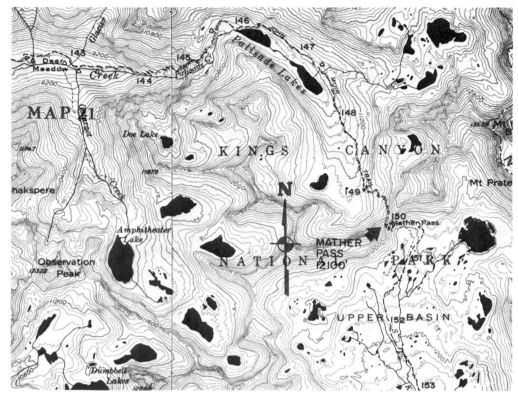

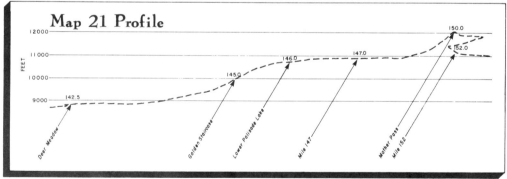

Map 21 Profile

savor the panorama. From here it includes an overview of Upper Basin and the South Fork of the Kings River drainage as far south as Mt. Brewer. Stephen Mather was the first director (beginning in 1916) of the National Park Service. Appropriately, the next pass you'll cross was named for Gifford Pinchot, the first head of the U.S. Forest Service when it was transferred

to the Department of Agriculture in 1905.

Wind down the southeast-facing slope in nine switchbacks, and then traverse to the east before making the final four short turns down to the floor of **Upper Basin.** Walk across the tundra, passing near a few tarns, to a lateral moraine and descend gradually along its crest. Although the grass cover never be-

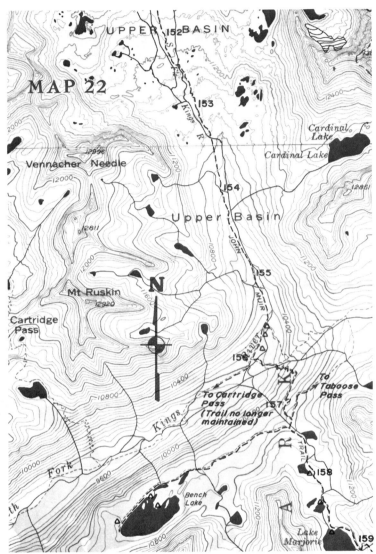

MAP 22

UPPER BASIN

Cardinal Lake

Vennacher Needle

Upper Basin

Mt Ruskin

Cartridge Pass

N

To Cartridge Pass
(Trail no longer maintained)

To Taboose Pass

Kings

Fork

Bench Lake

Lake Marjorie

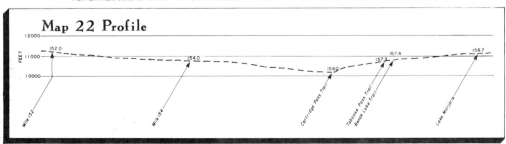

Map 22 Profile

comes luxuriant, the scene is most pleasing. Finally cross the first stream at 153.4 miles and farther on pass the first trees. Cross three more flows and descend through an attractive stretch of meadows and conifers. Cross another stream, and 0.3 mile father look left for the first good camp area. More sites are farther down the trail.

Come to a sign indicating the way to Bench Lake and Pinchot Pass. The obscure, unmaintained trail to Cartridge Pass heads west (right) here. Turn left and continue a few hundred feet down to the ford of the **South Fork of the Kings River.** From this point it's all uphill to Pinchot Pass. Beyond the ford cross a side stream and then climb steeply for a short distance. Switchback

up at a more moderate grade and traverse a slope of rocks and small pines. You can look back to Mather Pass and Upper Basin that you've recently descended. After one more brief stretch of steepish grade continue in woods to a sign pointing back to Mather Pass. The unsigned route to the left is the exit trail over Taboose Pass.

The trail to Taboose Pass, occasionally faint from here to the crest, rises through a lush basin generously sprinkled with wild flowers for 2.5 miles with 1,050 feet of elevation gain to the complex pass area. The downhill section of the trail on the east side is along a good tread. This exit is exceptionally scenic for the first two-thirds of the distance, but it ends at a less-frequented roadhead 5.0 miles off U.S. 395.

SECTION G

SOUTH FORK OF THE KINGS RIVER TO WOODS CREEK

The climb from the South Fork of the Kings River over Pinchot Pass and down past Twin Lakes to Woods Creek is, in its straightforwardness, a first cousin to the previous section over Mather Pass. The similarities stop there. The many lakes on the north side of Pinchot Pass and the staircase of little basins carpeted with grass and uncounted tarns on the south create an effect considerably less imposing than the terrain flanking its northern relative.

Side Trip. Just beyond the junction of the Taboose Pass Trail at 156.0 miles you can make a 1.3-mile side trip to Bench Lake. The first part of this spur is obscure, so be prepared to search a bit for the tread.

Exit. The exit over Sawmill Pass at 164.3 miles is a brother to the one over Taboose Pass, except the Sawmill route is even less used although it has a more reasonable grade and passes several lakes. The ultra adventuresome should note that no cross-country travel above 11,000 feet is permitted east of the JMT between Sawmill Pass and Dragon Pass above the Rae Lakes basin. This restriction is to protect the bighorn sheep that roam the area.

Camping Restrictions. Only gas stoves are allowed at Twin Lakes.

Keep right at the junction of the Taboose Pass Trail, abruptly leave the woods, and cross the exit creek from Lake Marjorie.

If you intend to visit Bench Lake, 1.3 miles to the southwest, veer right from the JMT several yards beyond the stream. Pick up the trail tread, reenter woods, de-scend, losing 200 feet of elevation, to more open terrain, and walk the final distance, crossing two streams. Many good campsites are along the north and east shores.

Rise gradually through a delicate alpine setting. Pass above the lowest lake in the Lake Marjorie complex, then cross the outlet from a lake on your right that is obscured by a low ridge. A few good campsites are nestled beneath the stunted trees between the trail and this lake near its southern end. These are the last sheltered spots on the north side of the pass. Cross two streams, pass a third lake, and wind uphill among rocks to **Lake Marjorie**. Walk above the lake and resume wending your way up along a slope of grass, rocks, and a few stunted trees. Farther on you can look down onto a small lake that has been dammed by a moraine.

Rise above timberline to a basin well populated with marmots. Cross the bowl at a gradual grade, then continue more sharply uphill until you have a view over a final body of water about as large as Lake Marjorie at the base of a red-colored wall. Make several short switchbacks near a stream, the last source of water for 1.5 miles, and eventually cross it. Wind up the rocky trail that, for many, has a grade just a bit too steep for establishing a methodical pace — fortunately, an uncommon characteristic of the JMT. As you climb higher you can see over the entire Lake Marjorie chain. The hard work necessary to reach 12,100-foot **Pinchot Pass** will be rewarded with spectacular views that extend south over a lake-filled basin to Mt. Cedric Wright and beyond to Forester Pass on the far

58

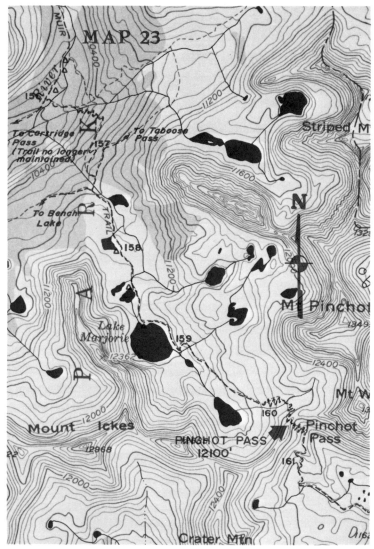

MAP 23

To Cartridge Pass
(Trail no longer maintained)

To Taboose Pass

To Bench Lake

Striped Mt

N

Mt Pinchot

Lake Marjorie

Mount Ickes

Pinchot Pass

PINCHOT PASS
12100'

Crater Mtn

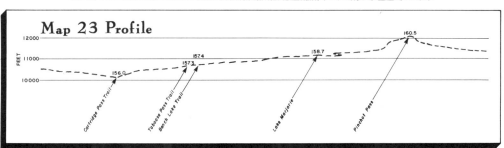

Map 23 Profile

12000
11000
10000

FEET

160.5

157.4

158.7

156.0
157.3

Cartridge Pass Trail
Taboose Pass Trail
Bench Lake Trail
Lake Marjorie
Pinchot Pass

Lake Marjorie

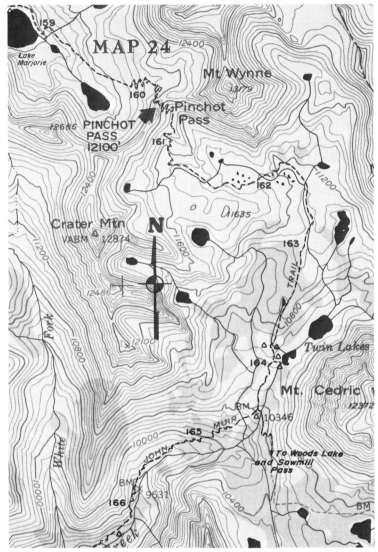

MAP 24

Lake Marjorie

159

12400

Mt Wynne

13179

160

Pinchot Pass

12685

PINCHOT PASS 12100'

161

162

1635

Crater Mtn

VABM △ 12874

163

N

11200

11600

TRAIL

10800

12486

Fork

×12100

10800

Twin Lakes

164

White

Mt. Cedric

12372

BM △ 10346

10000

165

MUIR

To Woods Lake and Sawmill Pass

BM

JOHN

BM

166

×9631

10400

BM

Creek

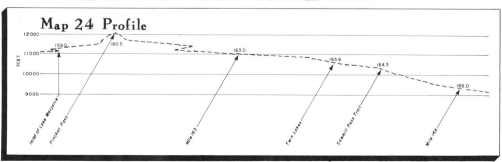

Map 24 Profile

FEET

12000

11000

159.0

160.5

10000

9000

163.0

163.9

164.3

166.0

Inlet of Lake Marjorie — Pinchot Pass — Mile 163 — Twin Lakes — Sawmill Pass Trail — Mile 166

Looking north from Pinchot Pass, Lake Marjorie and Mt. Ruskin in background

horizon. To the north is the terrain you've covered since Mather Pass. The pass itself is not visible, but the Palisades beyond it are obvious, and the view continues north as far as Mt. Goddard.

Wind steeply down the rocky trail before descending at a more knee-pleasing angle. Climb briefly, then resume the downhill, and come to the tundra line. Pass a couple of tarns, wind down through the typically lovely scene to a basin filled with more wee lakes, hop an outlet, and drop to a second, smaller bowl. Cross a soggy area of rock slabs, and wander down to the third, largest, and prettiest basin. Continue to the end of a lake and cross its outlet. Gradually descend along the tundra that is now sprinkled with scat-tered boulders and trees. Climb slightly and then drop into the final basin, also with a lake at its end.

Walk beside the length of the lake, resume descending, and soon have a view down over **Twin Lakes.** Farther on come to sign marking the spur to the lakes and the many campsites there. Remember: Gas stoves only at Twin Lakes. Continue down for 0.4 mile to where an old sign on the right reads *John Muir Trail.* To reach a good campsite, turn left here, cross one branch of **Woods Creek,** and then turn right.

The trail past the above campsite crosses the other branch of Woods Creek and continues for 3.0 miles with 1,000 feet of elevation gain to Sawmill Pass. It then descends for 9.0 miles to a roadhead 4.0 miles west of U.S. 395.

WOODS CREEK TO BULLFROG LAKE

The Rae Lakes Basin, whose length you'll traverse before you climb over Glen Pass, is one of those extra special places in the High Sierra. Depending on whether you prefer crispness or softness, the basin is at its prime either in the early morning or late in the evening just before sunset. Photographers will lament that they can't pack all their heavy artillery and do full justice to the scene.

The serpent in this paradise is accessibility. Masses of hikers take advantage of the approaches — from the east over Glen and Kearsarge passes and from the west out of Cedar Grove. If possible, try to travel on a weekday through the stretch between the Woods Creek crossing at 168.0 miles and Vidette Meadow at 179.5 miles.

Side Trip. A highly recommended digression is to the Sixty Lakes Basin from the southwest end of the Rae Lakes Basin. This side trip could be as much as 3.5 miles (one-way) with 640 feet of uphill. The scenery warrants five times the effort.

Exits. You can exit west from the 167.9-mile point for 17.0 miles down Woods Creek through Paradise Valley to Cedar Grove. Three routes head east. One is over Baxter Pass and begins from Dollar Lake at the north end of the Rae Lakes Basin. The portion of the route up to the pass may be a bit obscure, but from the crest down the east side the tread is obvious. The second is a difficult cross-country route over Dragon Pass to Onion Valley, starting from the southeast end of the basin. Definitely the easiest way is the third exit over Kearsarge Pass from

the 177.5-mile point. Actually, the elevation gain is about the same for all three exits, but the one over Kearsarge has the best-defined tread and grade.

Camping Restrictions. Because of heavy use along this section, camping restrictions are numerous. A one-day camp limit is imposed at all sites between the Woods Creek crossing at 168.0 miles and Charlotte Lake on the south side of Glen Pass. Gas stoves only are permitted in the Rae Lakes Basin. If you intend to exit over Kearsarge Pass, note that gas stoves only are allowed on both sides of the pass, there's a one-day limit at Kearsarge Lakes, and Bullfrog Lake is closed to all camping.

Unfortunately, bears patrol from the Woods Creek crossing through the Rae Lakes Basin and in the Charlotte Lake area, so observe the proper precautions for storing food.

From the junction of the trail to Sawmill Pass, continue downhill, cross a good-sized side stream, and descend more steeply. Pass some smatterings of aspen and enter the narrow, deep, rocky, and sometimes very hot, gorge holding Woods Creek. This stretch of sage and other scrubby vegetation is seen nowhere else along the JMT, although the mixture is common at the lower elevations on some of the routes on the eastern slopes of the Sierra. The grade, overall, now becomes less severe, and the few brief uphill sections are a welcome change. Cross a small side stream and soon travel on the level past a campsite to your left. Resume descending for a few tenths of a mile,

Small waterfall on Woods Creek

cross a good-sized stream, and then go through the signed White Fork Drift Fence. Continue downhill 1.2 miles, crossing four side streams, to the valley floor and the junction of the Woods Creek Trail to Cedar Grove.

This exit is mostly gradual downhill for the 17.0 miles to Cedar Grove. It forms the northern leg of the popular Rae Lakes loop that, after traversing the Rae Lakes Basin and crossing Glen Pass, returns to Cedar Grove along Bubbs Creek.

Turn left, pass a camp area, and cross Woods Creek on a footbridge. More campsites are off to the right. Although these are adequate, the ones in the Rae Lakes Basin are far more pleasing aesthetically. Begin the 3.0-mile, 1,800-foot climb to the north end of the basin. Although not lush or alpine in character, the canyon of the **South Fork of Woods Creek** has a far less arid appearance than the one you just came down. After 1.0 mile come to a wide, shallow stream and continue uphill at a comfortable grade. Cross a little meadow, then wind up a rocky ridge, and from its crest drop to the Baxter Drift Fence and cross a stream, the last source of water until Rae Lakes Basin. **Baxter Creek,**

Campsite at the Rae Lakes

by the way, is the large flow across the canyon. Climb the final mile through a more characteristic Sierra landscape of rocks, grass, and scattered trees to **Dollar Lake.** There are good campsites near the northwest shore and a pit toilet to the north above the trail. From Dollar Lake you'll have your first views of impressive Fin Dome, the Painted Lady, and the other peaks at the head of the basin.

The initially obscure exit route over Baxter Pass crosses the outlet from Dollar Lake and heads northeast. After gaining 2,150 feet in 4.5 miles to Baxter Pass,

the route becomes well defined and loses 6,300 feet in 7.9 miles. The 5.5-mile road from the moderately popular trailhead meets U.S. 395 2.0 miles north of Independence.

Walk above the west shore of Dollar Lake, climb a short distance, and cross the outlet from **Arrowhead Lake** on a log. Walk parallel to, but a couple of hundred feet from, the east side of Arrowhead Lake. Remember to establish any camp at least 100 feet from shoreline. Climb for 0.3 mile, level off, and travel above the lowest of the three **Rae Lakes.** A toilet is upslope

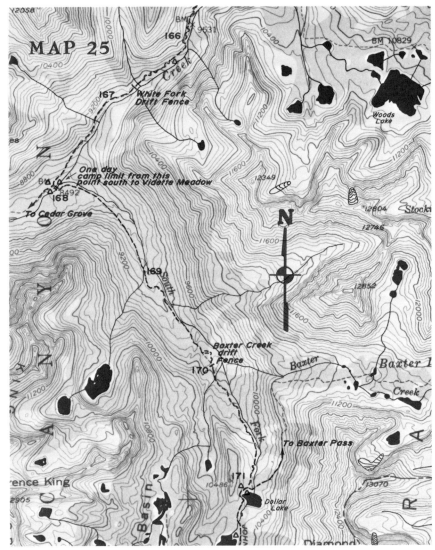

MAP 25

Woods Lake

White Fork Drift Fence

One day camp limit from this point south to Vidette Meadow

To Cedar Grove

Baxter Creek drift Fence

To Baxter Pass

Dollar Lake

Diamond

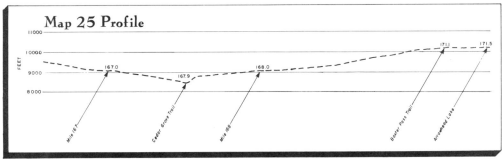

Map 25 Profile

Cascade on Woods Creek

Fin Dome from the Rae Lakes Basin

here and another is near the northeast end of the highest lake. Traverse above the middle lake, crossing many small side streams, with a particularly pungent patch of wild onion along one short stretch. You can see Glen Pass ahead to the southwest. It's the ridge that's topped by a darker band of rock. For those heading south, the ranger station is obscure. If you need to visit it, turn around occasionally after you've passed the midpoint of the second Rae Lake. The light-colored canvas tent is easy to spot when looking north.

Adventuresome hikers who want to exit to Onion Valley could follow the possibly unsigned route up Dragon Creek to Dragon Lake, then cross-country past three more lakes to Dragon Pass. From there descend to Golden Trout Lake and the upper end of a trail that continues down to Onion Valley. You should view this as an interesting and challenging option, not as a shortcut, as the elevation gain and the time needed are about the same as for the conventional exit over Kearsarge Pass. A reminder: Cross-country travel east of the JMT and above 11,000 feet between Dragon and Sawmill passes is prohibited.

Walk along a grassy inner valley out of sight of any of the lakes, then travel the length of the isthmus that separates the upper two lakes, and cross the outlet from the upper one. About 200 feet farther you reach the junction of the trail to Sixty Lakes Basin.

The hike to the southern end of lovely Sixty Lakes Basin is 2.0 miles with 640 feet of uphill, but a trail continues another few miles north into the valley. Conies and marmots are almost as plentiful as the plethora of lakes.

Keep left and begin winding uphill. The initially steep grade soon becomes more moderate. Plenty of water is available until you come to the last stream at the abrupt end of vegetation. Climb steeply up a rubbly ridge for a short distance, then travel at a moderate grade for a view down onto a tarn. Descend among barren rock masses to the wall directly below the pass and begin switchbacking uphill. As you gain elevation you can see more tarns below you and, eventually, the Rae Lakes. The tread is rocky and, although not agonizingly severe, it is overall the steepest pass climb along the JMT. Finally, arrive at the very narrow crest at 11,978-foot **Glen Pass.** If you stand on a rock just above the trail you can spot Forester Pass, the next high point to cross.

Walk along the knife-edged crest, then begin switchbacking down into a cliff-walled bowl. Although the tread is smoother than on the north side, it is no less steep. Pass above a large tarn, then near a smaller one — the last source of water for 2.1 miles. Descend through an attractive little rocky canyon to the junction of a route down to camping areas at Charlotte Lake.

This side excursion lies along the north shore and then climbs back to the JMT, meeting the latter at its 177.7-mile point. Visiting Charlotte Lake would involve an additional 300 feet of uphill but little extra mileage.

Climb briefly, then travel high above **Charlotte Lake** along a rocky slope that supports some small pines. Traverse down and come to the junction of the first of three possible approaches to Kearsarge Pass, the easiest exit over a pass along the JMT.

Assuming you're doing the JMT from north to south, this high trail is the preferred route over Kearsarge Pass, since you lose no elevation. Climb for 3.5 miles with 1,000 feet of uphill. Along the way enjoy a bird's-eye view over Bullfrog and then Kearsarge lakes. The small pass at 11,800 feet is more like a notch on the side of a peak. Descend 5.0 miles, losing 2,600 feet, to Onion Valley, one of the three most popular access points on the east side of the Sierra.

Keep right and continue downhill for 0.1 mile to a flat clearing of pumice and a four-way junction. The route on the right comes from Charlotte Lake; the trail to the left across the open area climbs to the high trail over Kearsarge

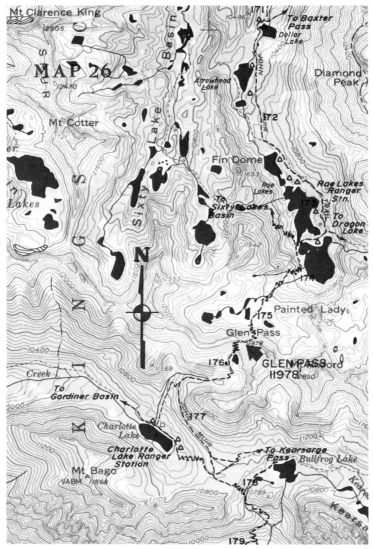

MAP 26

Mt Clarence King
12905

Mt Cotter

Sixty Lake Basin

Fin Dome

Arrowhead Lake

To Baxter Pass
Dollar Lake

Diamond Peak

Rae Lakes

Rae Lakes Ranger Stn.

To Sixty Lakes Basin

173

To Dragon Lake

174

N

175   Painted Lady

Glen Pass

1978

176   GLEN PASS 11978'

Creek

To Gardiner Basin

177

Charlotte Lake

Charlotte Lake Ranger Station

Mt Bago
VABM 11868

To Kearsarge Pass   Bullfrog Lake

178

Kearsarge

179

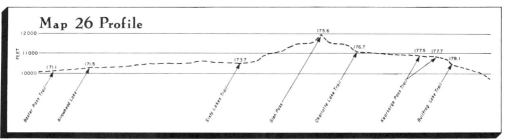

Map 26 Profile

12000

11000

FEET

10000

171.1   Baxter Pass Trail
171.5   Arrowhead Lake
173.7   Sixty Lakes Trail
Glen Pass
175.6
176.7   Charlotte Lake Trail
177.5   Kearsarge Pass Trail
177.7   Bullfrog Lake Trail
178.1

Pass. Keep straight, continue mostly on the level with a few minor ups and downs to a notch, then wind down to the junction of the trail to Bullfrog Lake.

This third way to approach Kearsarge Pass climbs to attractive Bullfrog Lake, skirts the north shore, and resumes rising to the junction with the short spur to the Kearsarge Lakes. The trail continues up and joins the high trail 1.0 mile below the pass.

Upper Rae Lake and Dragon Peak

BULLFROG LAKE TO TYNDALL CREEK

Ever upward. The high point along this section is the narrow — both in width and length — notch of Forester Pass, the second highest pass along the JMT. Upcoming Trail Crest is number one.

Side Trips. For those disposed to side trips, definitely make the one that leaves the JMT at 182.4 miles and climbs through Center Basin to Junction Pass. If you desire a reference for the area's merit, refer to the cover photo of that beautiful book, *Sierra Nevada — The Gentle Wilderness.* To camp at Golden Bear Lake near the west end of the basin and then make a leisurely hike up to Junction Pass would be a delightful semi-rest day.

Another excellent side trip to an even less-frequented area is the loop into Lake South America and Milestone Basin from the 191.3-mile point.

Exits. You can exit west to Cedar Grove at 179.0 miles; also west to Giant Forest or Wolverton from 191.7 miles, a short distance beyond the Tyndall Creek crossing.

Camping Restrictions. There are no special camping restrictions, and, to date, bears have not been a problem beyond Vidette Meadow.

From the junction of the trail to Bullfrog Lake continue winding downhill in woods, crossing and recrossing a small stream, and after 1.0 mile come to the junction of the southern route to Cedar Grove.

After 15 miles of gradual descent, this exit meets the trail that left the JMT just before the crossing of Woods Creek at

167.9 miles, then continues the remaining 2.0 miles to the roadhead.

Keep left, and in a short distance keep straight at a connector to the route to Cedar Grove, then travel at a gradual uphill grade, crossing three side streams. The woods become more open and the ground cover more rocky. Wind uphill for 0.3 mile and then resume traversing along the valley wall. **East Vidette Peak** is the mountain to the west, and the **Kearsarge Pinnacles** form the crest along the east wall directly above you. Arrive at the East Vidette Drift Fence and continue uphill to a more meadowy scene. Descend slightly, pass a large camp area, and travel through more open woods to a sign identifying the John Muir Trail and listing a few mileages to the north and south. The unsigned path that heads left (east) goes to Center Basin and Junction Pass.

To make this very scenic side trip, climb (with a few level stretches farther on) along the rough tread for 1.5 miles with 600 feet of uphill to the edge of the basin. Walk along a rocky area with a granular surface to a large tarn. It involves only a little detective work to discover where the cover photo for the *Gentle Wilderness* was taken. Climb a low ridge to timberline and arrive above the northwest end of Golden Bear Lake.

Prior to construction of the JMT over Forester Pass, the route over the Kings-Kern Divide was through Center Basin and over Junction and Shepherd passes. You can exit to the east along this old route. Since the Shepherd Pass Trail also continues west to the JMT, joining it at the 191.5-mile point, you also can make a side loop through Center Basin and over Junction and Shepherd passes. The exit or side loop is for experienced backpackers

71

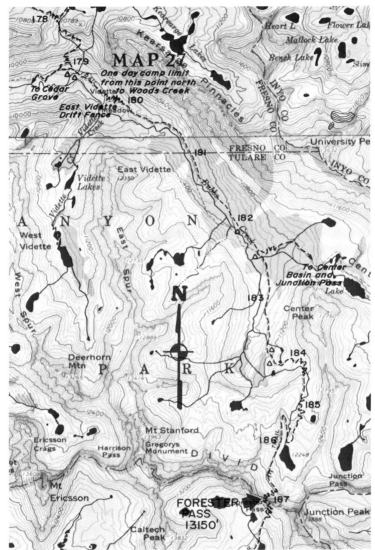

MAP 27

One day camp limit
from this point north
to Woods Creek

To Cedar
Grove

East Vidette
Drift Fence

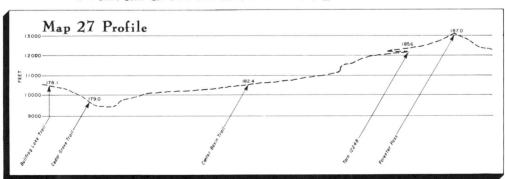

Map 27 Profile

Bubbs Creek and Junction Peak

Melting snowfield south of Forester Pass

only, as the tread may be obscure in places. However, establishing a camp near Golden Bear Lake and making a day hike up to Junction Pass is highly recommended for everyone.

To reach Junction Pass (it's on the summit of a wide block just to the left of pyramid-shaped Junction Peak — not the saddle between the two) continue along the trail for about 200 yards beyond the southeast end of Golden Bear Lake. Look right for a pyramid-shaped granite boulder in the middle of the flat grassy area and a faint tread heading south about 150 yards to the east of the rock. Drop slightly and cross the inlet stream and the grass. Initially the trail is not well defined as it winds up around rocks and bushes. Cross a stream, traverse along a moraine on a now-obvious path, and make two switchbacks to the top of the wall forming the southern end of Center Basin. Travel up

Marmot

above a large, unnamed lake, then traverse a rocky slope, and climb in switchbacks to the ridge top. As you walk south along this crest you can look down into upper Bubbs Creek valley and across to Forester Pass and portions of the trail leading to it. As you will discover, the terrain below Forester Pass is much more complex and interesting than it appears from here. Cross a broad saddle. Climb in switchbacks and traverses, passing many clusters of the exceedingly fragrant polemonium, to Junction Pass, with spectacular views in all directions.

Continue gradually uphill through woods, crossing **Center Basin Creek.** Make one set of switchbacks and come to an open, bushy slope. Wind and traverse up across it to a zone of pine. Just before timberline, pass a large

75

camp area on your right, the last sheltered one until Tyndall Creek at 191.5 miles. Walk through an attractive, grassy bench and beyond it begin winding up over boulder-strewn terrain. At 184.3 miles cross one of the streams that comprise the headwaters of Bubbs Creek, wind up to another basin, climb through it, and travel above a tarn. Rise above the last patches of grass and make many short switchbacks, pass another tarn, then begin a long traverse. Travel just above an austere, crystal-clear pool and walk on the level to near the north end of a good-sized lake. From here you'll be able to look directly up to Forester Pass.

Traverse north along a steep, rocky slope, climb to a ridge, and begin winding up along its crest. You'll be able to see down onto many lakes and tarns, down Bubbs Creek canyon, and across to Junction Pass. Make two switchbacks, traverse to the base of the wall, then wind up in seventeen short switchbacks to 13,150-foot **Forester Pass**, which is small and narrow. Fortunately, this final 1.4 miles has a good grade and, besides the view, you'll again be treated to the rich scent of polemonium (also called sky pilot) if you make the climb during its relatively short blooming season. Although this particular member of the Phlox family grows only from 13,000 to 14,000 feet (and tends to be a bit fussy about its location even within that lofty realm) where it does grow it thrives abundantly. From the pass, which forms the boundary of **Kings Canyon and Sequoia national parks,** you can see down onto the lakes you'll soon pass, to Kern Canyon, east along the Kings-Kern Divide, and southwest to the Kaweah Peaks.

Switchback down the sheer south wall of the pass to the floor of a barren, lake-filled basin — the most bleak scene since the north side of Muir Pass. At the south end of the basin wend your way down over a rocky scarp. You can look southeast to the Bighorn Plateau,

which you'll cross in 5.0 miles. Continue down through a large bowl where you'll encounter the first grasses and also many marmots. The spire to the left is Mt. Tyndall. Descend through another basin, pass a lake below on your left, and soon you'll be able to spot the shelter on the summit of Mt. Whitney. Enter a third basin and travel high along the shoulder of the big valley holding Tyndall Creek. From here you can look up toward Shepherd Pass. The grass becomes denser, a cluster of trees is an overture to timberline, and then, after a last open stretch, the woods begin.

Just below timberline, pass the signed junction on your right of the trail to Lake South America and Milestone Basin. (After 0.6 mile the trail forks, with one branch going to Lake South America and the other directly to Milestone Basin. The route to the lake eventually loops back to Milestone Creek, so a one-way circuit is possible.)

Keep straight, after ninety yards approach **Tyndall Creek,** and after sixty yards ford it. Although you'll get your feet and lower legs wet, the crossing is normally no problem. If the campsites here are not to your liking, there are a few more farther along the JMT. About 100 yards beyond the creek, watch for an unsigned path heading off to your left. This is the route up to Shepherd and Junction passes. (The exit over Shepherd Pass climbs 1,150 feet in 3.5 miles and then loses 6,400 feet as it drops for 9.0 miles to the Symmes Creek roadhead 7.0 miles from U.S. 395.)

One hundred yards or so farther along the JMT, pass more campsites and arrive at the junction of the trail to the Kern River Canyon and Junction Meadow. If you want to exit to Giant Forest or Wolverton, this is the most efficient route out. A summer ranger station is located 0.5 mile down this trail.

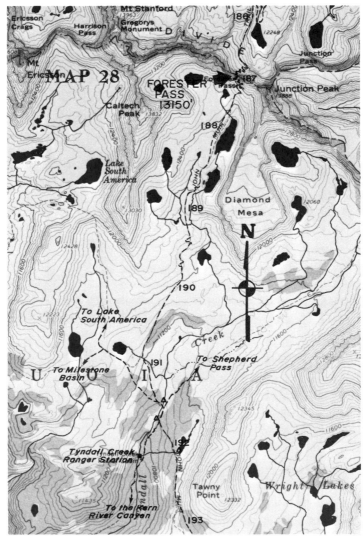

MAP 28

Ericsson
Crags

Mt Stanford
13963

Harrison
Pass

Gregorys
Monument

D · I · V · I · D · E

186

12248

Mt
Ericsson

Junction
Pass

FORESTER
PASS
13150'

Forester
Pass

187

Junction Peak
13888

Caltech
Peak
13832

188

Lake
South
America

189

Diamond
Mesa
12060

N

13030

12428

190

12223

To Lake
South America

Creek

To Shepherd
Pass

U · O · I · A

191

To Milestone
Basin

12345

192

Tyndall Creek
Ranger Station

Tawny
Point
12332

Wright Lakes

To the Kern
River Canyon

193

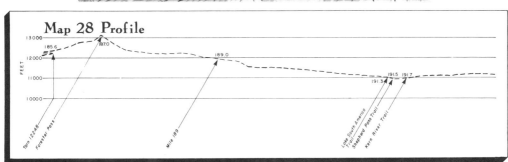

Map 28 Profile

TYNDALL CREEK TO WHITNEY PORTAL

This last section is reminiscent of the alignment of the JMT north of Muir Pass. It follows a more complex route, which is actually a nice balance after the tidy, repeated ups and downs over the four previous passes.

Side Trip. It would be the odd soul who didn't want to make the 2.1-mile side trip from the 205.4-mile point to the summit of Mt. Whitney. As you already know from an earlier sighting, the summit area is well away from other peaks, so the view is panoramic. Among many other landmarks, you'll see signs of civilization in the Owens Valley below to the east. Perhaps this isn't a welcome sight, but it will prepare you for the offenses to your sensibilities as you head down amidst a stream of people on the trail to Whitney Portal. The main difference between the hordes here and the ones you encountered at the north end of the JMT is that many of these hikers are obviously suffering from the effort and the altitude as they push their unprepared bodies to that magical mountaintop.

Exit. You can make the long exit west from the 196.0-mile point just before

Timberline Lake and the west side of Mt. Whitney

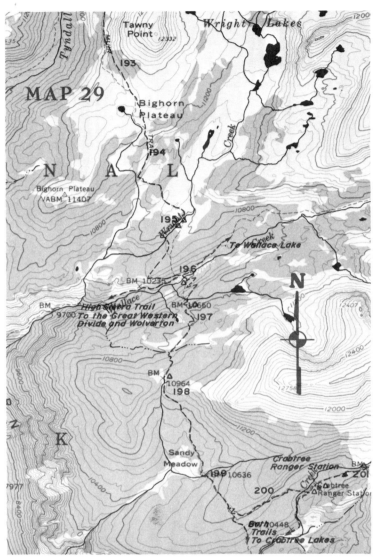

MAP 29

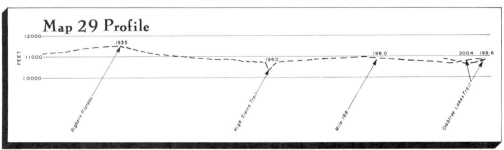

Map 29 Profile

crossing Wallace Creek along the High Sierra Trail. This route eventually connects with the exit at Tyndall Creek and ends at Giant Forest.

If weather permits, you should camp as high as possible in the basin on the west side of Trail Crest, specifically in the Guitar Lake area or just above a higher tarn. You'll want to be able to make the 4.5-mile, 3,000-foot climb to the summit of Mt. Whitney and then get over Trail Crest and down to timberline before any thunderstorms let loose. If you must camp on the east side, be forewarned that Trail Camp can be the slum of the Sierra. Outpost Camp at 209.8 miles may be a better choice. This is not meant to criticize the Forest Service — it's just that most of the hikers on the trail are intent only on climbing Mt. Whitney, and too many of them have bad outdoor manners. Fortunately, few of them have the desire or stamina to go deeper into the backcountry.

Camping Restrictions. No camping is allowed at Timberline Lake. Gas stoves are required from Guitar Lake all the way out along the JMT to Whitney Portal. On the east side, camping is prohibited at Trailside Meadow and Mirror Lake. Bears have invaded the Wallace Creek and Crabtree areas.

Keep left at the junction of the trail to the Kern River Canyon, climb moderately steeply, then pass a few good campsites just before crossing the outlet from a lake. Walk along the grassy floor of the bench that holds this unnamed lake, and then rise at an erratic grade through woods. Make one set of short switchbacks and continue up to treeless **Bighorn Plateau.** The seemingly lovely tarn off to the right supports a population of voracious mosquitoes. As you cross this fairly level expanse you'll have a second opportunity to spot the summit building on Mt. Whitney. Kern Ridge lies directly to the west.

Descend into a small bowl with a snow marker and wind down through rocky woods. Walk above a huge, verdant meadow, and travel across an area of lush grass and scattered boulders. Make a short, steep descent into the valley holding **Wrights Creek** and pass a fine camp area on your left between the trail and the stream. The ford of Wrights Creek farther on can be a bit difficult early in the season or immediately after a stormy period, so you might prefer to cross it in the meadow just above the tall trees. After this high crossing, parallel near the east side of the creek for about 0.1 mile to the JMT.

Beyond the crossing of Wrights Creek travel gradually downhill to the edge of the valley holding Wallace Creek, curve sharply left, and traverse down to the junction of the second exit to Giant Forest at 196.0 miles. This point is the east end of the **High Sierra Trail.**

Heading northeast from the junction is the unsigned 5.0-mile trail to Wallace Lake, with 1,050 feet of uphill. The route is obscure at first as it parallels Wallace Creek but becomes obvious farther on. A cross-country climb of 1,350 feet goes to Tulainyo Lake — at 12,802 feet the highest large lake in the contiguous United States. A short climb to the rim above this lake affords a spectacular view down into the Owens Valley.

Keep straight and ford **Wallace Creek.** Since the flow is very wide here, the crossing is not at all difficult. Campsites are located downstream on both sides of the creek. Walk upstream, climb in three switchbacks, level off, and cross a side creek. A possible campsite is off to the left just before the flow. Resume winding uphill and soon have a view back to the Bighorn Plateau. Cross a stream (which may not flow through the entire summer), travel on the level again, make a final climb to a saddle, and begin, except for one brief uphill stretch, the 2.5 miles of downhill or level grade to Whitney Creek.

Sandy Meadow and the Great Western Divide

Mt. Hitchcock

81

As you drop from the saddle you can see into the Kern River Canyon. Pass a meadow and descend gradually through woods that have completely changed character. Cross a few small streams, none of which are dependable sources of water, and travel along the upper edge of inclined **Sandy Meadow,** where you have an unobstructed view west to the Great Western Divide. Continue down for a couple of hundred feet to a tributary of Whitney Creek, climb,

walk on the level, then wind down to a junction. Up to this point the JMT from Tuolumne Meadows and the Pacific Crest Trail (the route that extends through the Pacific states from Canada to Mexico) have been contiguous. Here they part company, with the Pacific Crest Trail heading south and crossing Siberian Pass.

Keep left and continue downhill, with a peek at Crabtree Meadows, to an absolutely level sandy bench. As you

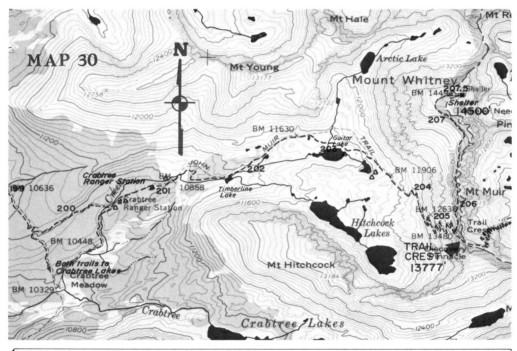

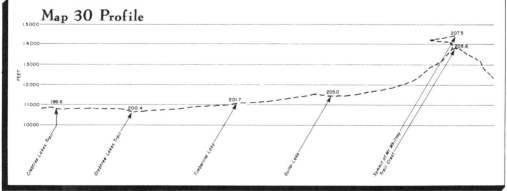

Looking northwest from the summit of Mt. Whitney

trudge across this stretch, your body will remind you how few times along the JMT it has walked on the level for any distance. Mt. Whitney is the peak ahead with the fluted face. Begin the more familiar motions of descending, pass a campsite near the edge of the woods, and drop through a lush meadow to the ford of **Whitney Creek.** This is one of the trickiest fords along the JMT, and even it is not particularly demanding.

On the opposite bank meet a connector down to the Pacific Crest Trail and Crabtree Lakes. Turn left and climb for several hundred feet to near the **Crabtree Ranger Station.** (The charming cabin that originally housed the ranger was replaced about ten years ago with an inappropriate modern structure.) Climb through woods for 0.4 mile to a small tarn and continue up to a meadow. Cross the stream on your left, immediately veer left, cross another fork, and pass a campsite.

Climb along an open slope to a bench and continue up a rocky wall. Travel high along the little gorge holding Whitney Creek, drop slightly, and walk near the north shore of **Timberline Lake,** where no camping is allowed. Climb steeply along a rocky stretch of trail, then rise more gradually through a swale of grass, rocks, and a stream. Climb to another swale that isn't as lush, and pass the last of the trees, that, by this elevation, are gnarled and stunted. Continue up the broad, massive valley to above **Guitar Lake,** then briefly climb steeply before dropping into a bowl with a tarn. Resume climbing to the last of the grass, water, and tolerable campsites. Assuming the weather is pleasant, the campsites here at the edge of the vegetation line are surprisingly hospitable.

If the snow hasn't completely melted you may have a little problem finding the route as it traverses up to the base of the wall. If necessary, look for people coming down from Trail Crest and watch where they leave the face. This obscure section is no longer than several hundred feet, and above it the route is of high standard. Wind uphill loosely, then methodically climb eighteen increasingly longer switchbacks. The grade is perfect for maintaining a good, steady pace, and the tread is smooth. As you gain elevation, you have ever-expanding views down onto

the Hitchcock Lakes, then higher up back over the valley to Timberline Lake, and even to Sandy Meadow. The wall directly to the west across the valley is Mt. Hitchcock. Three-tenths of a mile below Trail Crest on the east side you reach the junction of the spur to the summit of Mt. Whitney.

You're in such superb shape by now that the 2.1-mile, 900-foot climb seems like nothing more than a quick stroll. Turn left and continue uphill past Mt. Muir along the pinnacle-topped slope. Three-quarters of a mile below the summit, traverse past the cleavages near Day and Keeler Needles. From the narrow slits at each indentation you can peer almost 2,000 feet down onto small, unnamed tarns. Wind steeply uphill to the large, flat summit and the low stone hut that was built in 1909 as an astronomical observation station. Hopefully, it will be a warm, calm day so you can loll on the big, flat boulders and savor the view. The peak was named for Josiah Whitney, who was chief of the California State Geological Survey from 1860 to 1874 and who led survey parties into the Sierra during his tenure. The 14,450-foot peak was first climbed in 1873 by three men who started at Crabtree Meadows.

Keep straight, climb in a short set of switchbacks and come to 13,777-foot **Trail Crest** at the boundary of Sequoia National Park. East of here you will again be in the **John Muir Wilderness.** The views from the notch are extensive and include Owens Valley and the town of Lone Pine. Fragrant polemoniums thrive here, particularly on the east-facing slope just below the crest. Except for one bit of uphill beyond Outpost Camp, it's all downhill from here to Whitney Portal.

Make a long traverse to the east, begin winding down in approximately ninety, sometimes very short, switchbacks, and then walk on the level to **Trail Camp.** Despite the thousands of tromping feet here every season, the route for the next several hundred feet is not entirely obvious. As you did on the other side of Trail Crest, watch for people coming up. Even without them,

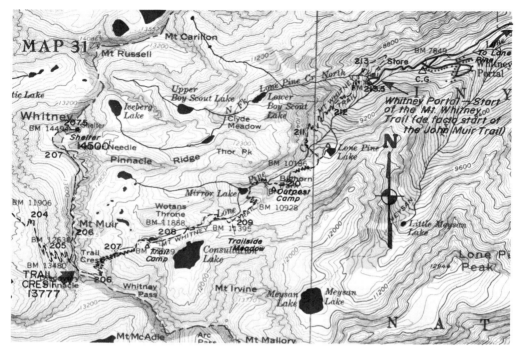

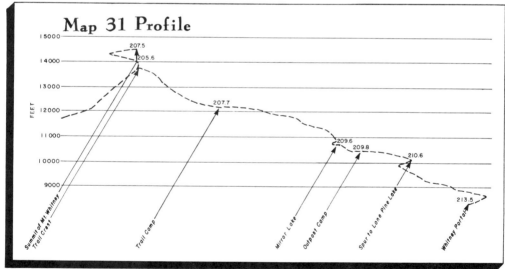

finding the correct route is not difficult, as the contours of the terrain funnel you onto the right course. Head over the rocks in a northeasterly direction, travel well above **Consultation Lake,** switchback once (you're on a well-defined trail by now), and cross a stream. Traverse along a rock wall, then wind down in erratically spaced switchbacks to a lovely little grassy swale identified as **Trailside Meadow.** This is a delightful spot for a final snack stop. No camping is permitted here.

Mirror Lake

Switchback five times, enjoy the view of Mirror Lake, and walk down along a broad crest. Switchback down its face, passing the first of the gnarled trees, and wind down the west slope of the ridge to near **Mirror Lake.** Cross the outlet, make one set of switchbacks to a decrepit bridge, have a view down onto the meadow area you'll be crossing, and continue descending in twelve switch-backs. The cover photo of this guide was taken along this stretch. Recross the outlet from Mirror Lake and walk to a sign identifying **Outpost Camp.** A toilet is a hundred feet or so to the right (south).

Continue on the level through a thicket of willow to a creek. The crossing at this point is very wide and shallow. Walk along the edge of a meadow

Outpost Camp and Wotans Throne

and climb — the very last uphill along the JMT — in two short switchbacks, then descend in fifteen switchbacks to a rocky canyon. Walk along its floor for 120 yards, and as you reenter woods pass the short spur to Lone Pine Lake that you peered down on before you reached timberline.

Meander down through woods along a trail that will be smooth for the remaining distance, and have a final crossing of **Lone Pine Creek**, the outlet from Mirror Lake. Make fourteen switchbacks, traverse, then make nine more, and pass a sign marking the boundary of the John Muir Wilderness. A couple of hundred feet beyond the sign, cross the **North Fork of Lone Pine Creek**. Descend in a long traverse, switchback, traverse a bit more, then make a couple of loose turns and come to **Whitney Portal Road.**

In many ways, the most difficult part about doing the JMT, or any trip in the Sierra, is leaving. On that final day you will have a bittersweet feeling, knowing that every step is taking you away from the scenery, the special sounds of the wilderness, the welcome warmth of the morning sun, the good, hard work and the relaxingly simple, regimented life, Well, better to have loved and left than never to have gone at all.

JOHN MUIR TRAIL MILEAGE AND ELEVATION STATISTICS TABLE

	ELEVATION in feet	MILEAGE North to South	MILEAGE South to North	DISTANCE BETWEEN in miles	ELEVATION CHANGE in feet +	−
Happy Isles	4,035	0.0	213.5			
				1.0	395	
Merced River Bridge	4,430	1.0	212.5			
				1.8	1,570	30
Glacier Point Trail	5,970	2.8	210.7			
				0.2		30
Nevada Fall	5,940	3.0	210.5			
				1.4	260	100
Little Yosemite Valley Ranger Station and Merced Lake Trail	6,100	4.4	209.1			
				1.7	900	
Half Dome Trail	7,000	6.1	207.4			
				0.5	200	
Clouds Rest Trail	7,200	6.6	206.9			
				1.3	560	
Sunrise Creek Crossing	7,760	7.9	205.6			
				1.2	340	
Tenaya Lake and Merced Lake Trails	8,100	9.1	204.4			
				0.9	300	
Sunrise Creek Crossing	8,400	10.0	203.5			
				3.4	1,460	500
Sunrise Lakes Trail	9,360	13.4	200.1			
				0.3	—	—
Sunrise High Sierra Camp	9,360	13.7	199.8			
				1.0	40	
Merced Lake Trail	9,400	14.7	198.8			
				2.6	550	250
Cathedral Pass	9,700	17.3	196.2			
				1.0		220
Lower Cathedral Lake Trail	9,480	18.3	195.2			
				2.3	100	680
Budd Lake Trail	8,900	20.6	192.9			
				0.9		260
Tuolumne Meadows Campground Trail	8,640	21.5	192.0			
				0.7		50
Soda Springs	8,590	22.2	191.3			
				0.7	10	
Young Lakes and Lembert Dome Trails	8,600	22.9	190.6			
				0.1	—	—

	ELEVATION in feet	MILEAGE North to South	MILEAGE South to North	DISTANCE BETWEEN in miles	ELEVATION CHANGE in feet +	ELEVATION CHANGE in feet −
Bridge over Highway 120	8,600	23.0	190.5			
				0.5	60	
Tuolumne Meadows Ranger Station	8,660	23.5	190.0			
				0.5	10	
Dana Fork Bridge	8,670	24.0	189.5			
				0.9	30	60
Lyell Fork Bridge	8,640	24.9	188.6			
				0.5	60	
Vogelsang Trail	8,700	25.4	188.1			
				4.2	180	
Evelyn and Ireland Lakes Trail	8,880	29.6	183.9			
				3.2	160	
Lyell Base Camp	9,040	32.8	180.7			
				1.3	660	
Lyell Fork Bridge	9,700	34.1	179.4			
				1.5	780	
Climbers' Route to Mt. Lyell....	10,480	35.6	177.9			
				1.4	626	50
Donohue Pass	11,056	37.0	176.5			
				2.5		1,056
Marie Lake Trail	10,000	39.5	174.0			
				0.8		350
Silver Lake Trail	9,650	40.3	173.2			
				1.3	550	
Island Pass	10,200	41.6	171.9			
				1.5		240
Agnew Pass Trail	9,960	43.1	170.4			
				0.1		10
Outlet of Thousand Island Lake	9,950	43.2	170.3			
				1.3	200	
Pass above Ruby Lake	10,150	44.5	169.0			
				1.0		390
Outlet of Garnet Lake	9,760	45.5	168.0			
				2.1		760
Lake Ediza Trail	9,000	47.6	165.9			
				0.7		220
Inlet of Shadow Lake	8,780	48.3	165.2			
				1.7	620	100
Rosalie Lake	9,300	50.0	163.5			
				0.8	400	
Gladys Pass	9,700	50.8	162.7			
				1.6		520
Trinity Lakes	9,180	52.4	161.1			
				1.7		1,060
Minaret Lake Trail	8,120	54.1	159.4			
				0.5		40
Beck Lakes Trail	8,080	54.6	158.9			
				1.2		530
Middle Fork Bridge............	7,550	55.8	157.7			
				0.2	30	30

	ELEVATION in feet	MILEAGE North to South	MILEAGE South to North	DISTANCE BETWEEN in miles	ELEVATION CHANGE in feet +	ELEVATION CHANGE in feet −
Devils Postpile National Monument	7,550	56.0	157.5			
				0.3	100	50
Rainbow Falls Trail	7,600	56.3	157.2			
				0.8	100	100
Rainbow Falls Trail	7,600	57.1	156.4			
				2.8	1,050	
Reds Meadow and Mammoth Pass Trails	8,650	59.9	153.6			
				1.2	430	
Mammoth Pass Trail	9,080	61.1	152.4			
				1.8	510	
Deer Lakes Trail	9,590	62.9	150.6			
				5.5	810	240
Duck Pass Trail	10,160	68.4	145.1			
				1.9	280	540
Fish Creek Trail at Purple Lake	9,900	70.3	143.2			
				1.9	600	300
Inlet at Lake Virginia	10,200	72.2	141.3			
				1.9	140	800
Tully Hole and McGee Pass Trail	9,540	74.1	139.4			
				1.5		440
Fish Valley Trail	9,100	75.6	137.9			
				1.9	1,160	
Squaw Lake	10,260	77.5	136.0			
				0.4	240	
Edison Lake Trail over Goodale Pass	10,500	77.9	135.6			
				0.3	30	
Chief Lake	10,530	78.2	135.3			
				0.8	370	
Silver Pass	10,900	79.0	134.5			
				1.0		540
Silver Pass Lake	10,360	80.0	133.5			
				2.8		1,360
Mott Lake Trail	9,000	82.8	130.7			
				0.2		120
Pocket Meadow	8,880	83.0	130.5			
				1.3		630
Mono Pass Trail	8,250	84.3	129.2			
				1.5		500
Edison Lake Trail	7,750	85.8	127.7			
				2.3	1,460	
First Water Source	9,160	88.1	125.4			
				2.3	820	
Bear Ridge Summit	9,980	90.4	123.1			
				0.9		380
Water Source	9,600	91.3	122.2			
				1.5		600
Bear Creek Trail	9,600	92.8	120.7			
				2.1	290	

	ELEVATION in feet	MILEAGE North to South	MILEAGE South to North	DISTANCE BETWEEN in miles	ELEVATION CHANGE in feet +	−
Lake Italy Trail	9,290	94.9	118.6			
				1.3	240	
Seven Gables Lakes Trail	9,530	96.2	117.3			
				1.2	430	
Rose Lake Trail	9,960	97.4	116.1			
				0.2	—	—
Sandpiper Lake Trail	9,960	97.6	115.9			
				1.4	640	
Marie Lake	10,600	99.0	114.5			
				0.9	260	
Selden Pass	10,860	99.9	113.6			
				0.7		310
Heart Lake	10,550	100.6	112.9			
				0.8		350
Sally Keyes Lakes	10,200	101.4	112.1			
				0.6		60
Unmaintained Trail to the South Fork	10,140	102.0	111.5			
				1.7		390
Senger Creek Crossing	9,750	103.7	109.8			
				2.2		1,350
Florence Lake Trail	8,400	105.9	107.6			
				1.5		510
Florence Lake Trail	7,890	107.4	106.1			
				1.8	255	100
Piute Pass Trail	8,045	109.2	104.3			
				3.1	485	150
South Fork Bridge	8,380	112.3	101.2			
				1.2	90	
Hell-For-Sure Pass Trail	8,470	113.5	100.0			
				1.7	790	
Evolution Creek Crossing	9,260	115.2	98.3			
				2.1	340	
McClure Meadow and Ranger Station	9,600	117.3	96.2			
				1.4	140	
Colby Meadow	9,740	118.7	94.8			
				2.0	920	
Lamarck Col Trail	10,660	120.7	92.8			
				0.6	190	
Evolution Lake	10,850	121.3	92.2			
				2.0	200	50
Sapphire Lake	11,000	123.3	90.2			
				2.0	500	
Outlet of Wanda Lake	11,500	125.3	87.9			
				2.0	455	
Muir Pass	11,955	127.3	86.2			
				1.1		155
Helen Lake Outlet	11,800	128.4	85.1			
				5.0		2,540
Big Pete Meadow	9,260	133.4	80.1			
				0.8		410

	ELEVATION in feet	MILEAGE North to South	MILEAGE South to North	DISTANCE BETWEEN in miles	ELEVATION CHANGE in feet +	ELEVATION CHANGE in feet −
Little Pete Meadow............	8,850	134.2	79.3			
				0.8		140
Bishop Pass Trail and Le Conte Ranger Station	8,710	135.0	78.5			
				2.7		510
Grouse Meadows	8,200	137.7	75.8			
				1.0	50	230
Tehipite Valley Trail	8,020	138.7	74.8			
				3.8	840	
Deer Meadow..................	8,860	142.5	71.0			
				2.5	1,540	
Golden Staircase	10,400	145.0	68.5			
				1.0	200	
Lower Palisade Lake	10,600	146.0	67.5			
				4.0	1,500	
Mather Pass...................	12,100	150.0	63.5			
				2.0		800
Head of Upper Basin	11,300	152.0	61.5			
				4.0		1,270
Cartridge Pass Trail	10,030	156.0	57.5			
				1.3	750	
Taboose Pass Trail	10,780	157.3	56.2			
				0.1	20	
Bench Lake Trail..............	10,800	157.4	56.1			
				1.3	360	
Lake Marjorie	11,160	158.7	54.8			
				1.8	940	
Pinchot Pass	12,100	160.5	53.0			
				3.4		1,500
Twin Lakes....................	10,600	163.9	49.6			
				0.4		250
Sawmill Pass Trail	10,350	164.3	49.2			
				3.6	1,855	
Cedar Grove Trail	8,495	167.9	45.6			
				0.1	—	—
Woods Creek Bridge	8,495	168.0	45.5			
				3.1	1,725	
Baxter Pass Trail at Dollar Lake	10,220	171.1	42.4			
				0.4	80	
Arrowhead Lake	10,300	171.5	42.0			
				1.6	350	50
Rae Lakes Ranger Station	10,600	173.1	40.4			
				0.2		40
Dragon Lake Trail.............	10,560	173.3	40.2			
				0.4		10
Sixty Lakes Basin Trail	10,550	173.7	39.8			
				1.9	1,428	
Glen Pass.....................	11,978	175.6	37.9			
				1.1		978
Charlotte Lake Trail	11,000	176.7	36.8			
				0.8		200

	ELEVATION in feet	MILEAGE North to South	MILEAGE South to North	DISTANCE BETWEEN in miles	ELEVATION CHANGE in feet +	ELEVATION CHANGE in feet −
Kearsarge Pass Trail	10,800	177.5	36.0			
				0.2		80
Kearsarge Pass Trail	10,720	177.7	35.8			
				0.4		220
Bullfrog Lake Trail	10,500	178.1	35.4			
				0.9		900
Cedar Grove Trail	9,600	179.0	34.5			
				0.5		50
Vidette Meadow	9,550	179.5	34.0			
				2.9	970	
Center Basin Trail	10,520	182.4	31.1			
				3.2	1,728	
Tarn 12248	12,248	185.6	27.9			
				1.4	902	
Forester Pass	13,150	187.0	26.5			
				4.3		2,180
Lake South America Trail	10,970	191.3	22.2			
				0.2		50
Ford of Tyndall Creek	10,920	191.5	22.0			
				0.0	—	—
Shepherd Pass Trail	10,920	191.5	22.0			
				0.2		40
Kern River Canyon Trail	10,880	191.7	21.8			
				1.8	550	
Bighorn Plateau	11,430	193.5	20.0			
				2.5		1,050
High Sierra Trail and Wallace Lake Trail	10,380	196.0	17.5			
				2.8	584	314
Sandy Meadow	10,650	198.8	14.7			
				0.8	220	
Crabtree Lakes Trail	10,870	199.6	13.9			
				0.8		240
Crabtree Lakes Trail	10,630	200.4	13.1			
				0.1	20	
Crabtree Ranger Station	10,650	200.5	13.0			
				1.2	450	
Timberline Lake	11,100	201.7	11.8			
				1.3	350	
Guitar Lake	11,450	203.0	10.5			
				2.4	2,150	
Junction of Mt. Whitney Trail	13,600	205.4	8.1			
				(2.1)	(900)	
Summit of Mt. Whitney official end of the John Muir Trail	(14,500)	(207.5)	(10.2)			
				0.2	177	
Trail Crest	13,777	205.6	7.9			
				2.1		1,737
Trail Camp	12,040	207.7	5.8			
				1.9		1,360

	ELEVATION in feet	MILEAGE North to South	MILEAGE South to North	DISTANCE BETWEEN in miles	ELEVATION CHANGE in feet +	−
Mirror Lake	10,680	209.6	3.9			
				0.2		315
Outpost Camp	10,365	209.8	3.7			
				0.8		265
Spur to Lone Pine Lake	10,100	210.6	2.9			
				2.9		1,750
Whitney Portal	8,350	213.5	0.0			

INDEX

97

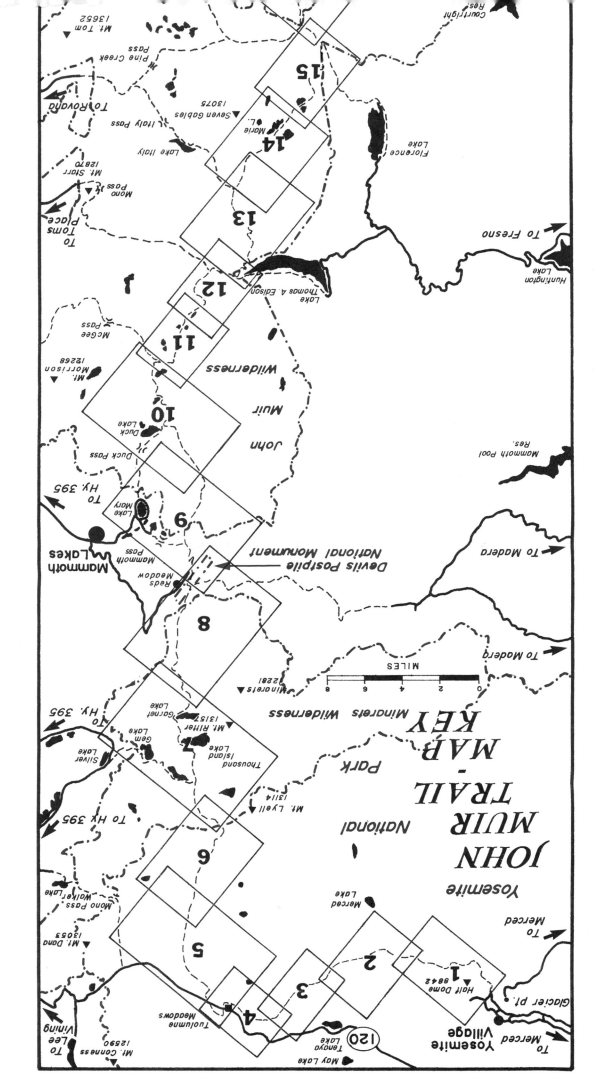

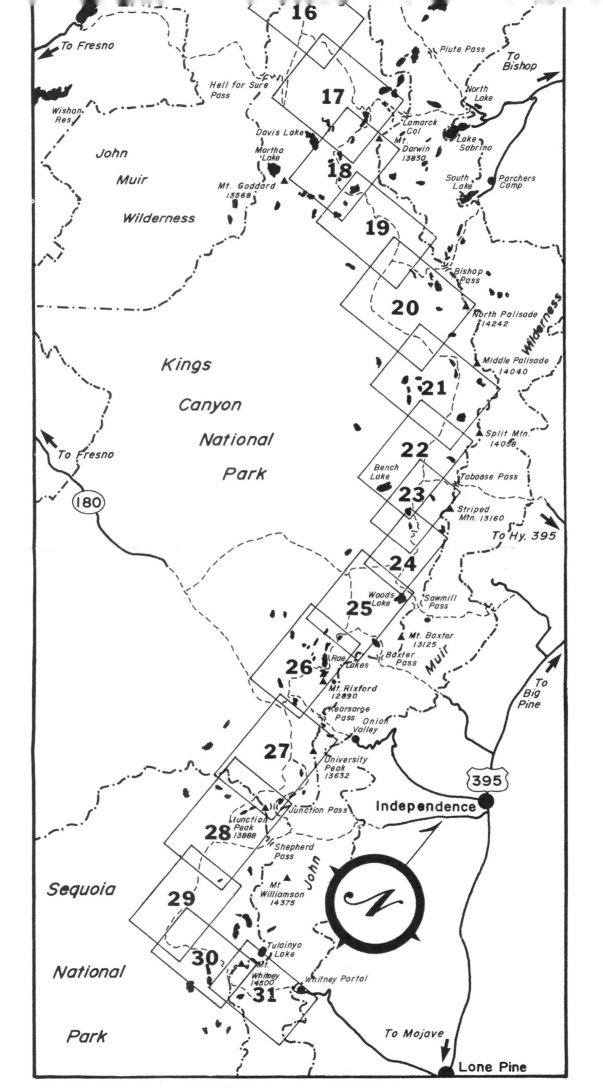